Contents

THE BATTLE
OF BARKING CREEK

THE TRUE STORY OF THE FIRST FATALLITY OF WORLD WAR TWO WHICH HAPPENED ON THE THIRD DAY OF WAR, IN WHAT WE WOULD NOW CALL A FRIENDLY FIRE INCIDENT.

ALL THE ACTION TAKES PLACE IN THE COURTROOM OF FIGHTER COMMAND AT BENTLEY PRIORY.

CHARACTER BREAKDOWN.

JUDGE ADVOCATE STIRLING SCOTTISH 52

AIR VICE MARSHAL CALLAWAY RP 47

PILOT OFFICER FREEBORN YORKSHIRE 19

AIR COMMODORE BENNINGTON RP 46

SIR PATRICK HASTINGS RP 49

COURT USHER LONDON 37

SQUADRON LEADER DONALDSON RP 33

PILOT OFFFICER ROSE RP 21

FLIGHT LIEUTENANT MALAN SOUTH AFRICAN 29

FLYING OFFICER BYRNE IRISH 20

GROUP CAPTAIN LUCKING RP 35

EXTERIOR OF THE COURTROOM AT BENTLEY PRIORY.

Sir Patrick Hastings.

> Hello Freeborn, how are you.

Pilot Officer Freeborn

> Not too bad Sir, thank you for asking….I'm sorry Sir, actually I'm pretty bloody, I've never been so scared in all my life.

Sir Patrick Hastings.

> I'm sure you are Freeborn old chap but bear up, we'll get you through this…on a wing and a prayer old boy, on a wing and a prayer.

Pilot Officer Freeborn

> Yes Sir, thank you Sir.

INTERIOR OF THE COURTROOM AT BENTLEY PRIORY.

Court Usher.
> SILENCE IN COURT

Judge Advocate Sterling

> Orders by Air Vice Marshal Keith Park dated 23rd September 1939, London.

> The detail of officers mentioned below will assemble at RAF Headquarters, Bentley Priory on 17th October 1939 for the purpose of trying by General Courts Martial the accused persons named in the margin.

> Air Vice Marshal William Callaway is appointed President.
> Members are Air Commodore Charles Widdows, Group Captain Nigel Norman and Group Captain Leonard Horwood.
> Mr C L Sterling that is myself is appointed Judge Advocate, Air Commodore Gerald Bennington is appointed for the prosecution and Sir Patrick Hastings is acting for the defence.

Air VM Callaway
> Pilot Officer Freeborn, do you object to being tried by me as President, or any of the other officers here before you.

Pilot Officer Freeborn
> No Sir.

Judge Advocate Sterling
> Have your rights under the rules of procedure been fully explained to you.

Pilot Officer Freeborn
> Yes Sir.

Judge Advocate Sterling
> Pilot Officer John Freeborn you are charged with insubordination, in that on the morning of 6th September you did cause the death of Pilot Officer Montague Hulton-Hurrop by attacking his aircraft, shooting him in the head, directly contradicting an order to cease the attack. Are you guilty or not guilty of the charge against you.

Pilot Officer Freeborn
> Not guilty.

Judge Advocate Sterling
> Air Commodore Bennington, does the prosecution wish to make an opening address.

Air Com Bennington
> Yes Sir. It is our case that on the morning of 6th September, only the third day after the declaration of war, that Pilot Officer Freeborn did shoot down and kill a fellow Officer… Pilot Officer Montague Hulton-Hurrop.
> It will be the case for the prosecution that this action was both reckless and foolhardy and in direct contradiction of an order to break off the attack
> We will hear testimony that on that fateful morning of the 6th at 06-15 hours a searchlight battery reported enemy aircraft flying in the vicinity of West Mersea, Essex.
> Sector operations at North Weald airfield received the report

and they contacted headquarters to say they had scrambled a flight of six Hurricane fighters from 56 Squadron to find the enemy aircraft.

All this took place in the space of twelve minutes, a very impressive performance I think you'll agree.

Amazingly by this time twenty raids had been plotted by Radar and fifty hostile aircraft had also been reported by 11 Group.

All the information pointed to a mass attack and to this end fighters from 151 Squadron, North Weald were scrambled and shortly after aircraft of 74, 54 and 65 Squadrons were scrambled from Hornchurch to join the search for the enemy.

Two pilots from 56 Squadron belatedly jumped into two reserve aircraft and flew after their comrades, flying some 1000 feet below and half a mile behind.

They were attacked by Pilot Officer Freeborn and Flying Officer Byrne of 74 Squadron in direct contradiction of an

order from their Flight Commander to break off when it was realised they were in fact attacking friendly aircraft.

Judge Advocate Sterling

Thank you Air Commodore Bennington, now Sir Patrick Hastings opening statement for the defence.

Sir Patrick Hastings

Whilst not disagreeing greatly with the prosecution about the facts leading up to the fateful event where Pilot Officer Hulton-Hurrop was shot down and killed.

I would like to point out that there was a great deal of confusion on the day, all of the sightings of enemy aircraft were later found to be false.

Serious errors were made that day but not by Pilot Officer Freeborn and Flying Officer Byrne who were both ordered to attack what they believed to be enemy aircraft and at no time did they receive an order to break off the attack.

Judge Advocate Sterling

Thank you Sir Patrick. Air Commodore Bennington do you wish to call your first witness.

Air Com Bennington

Yes Sir, I call Group Captain D F Lucking

Court Usher

Take the book in your right hand and repeat after me.

I swear by almighty God that the evidence I shall give before this court shall be the truth, the whole truth and nothing but the truth.

Group Captain Lucking

I swear by almighty God that the evidence I shall give before this court shall be the truth, the whole truth and nothing but the truth.

Air Com Bennington

Now, Group Captain you were Controller of Sector Operations at North Weald on the morning of the 6th and it was your responsibility to scramble the Squadrons at North Weald that day.

Group Captain Lucking

Yes Sir that's correct.

Air Com Bennington

Can you tell the court why so many aircraft were scrambled that day.

Group Captain Lucking

Well Sir, there weren't supposed to be so many, I only scrambled a Flight from 74 Squadron and was quite surprised to see the entire Squadron taking off.

Air Com Bennington

Why didn't you call them back when you realised too many aircraft were airborne.

Group Captain Lucking

The reports from HQ were constantly coming in suggesting there was a mass enemy attack so I took the decision that we would need all the aircraft we could muster to repel them.

Air Com Bennington

You say information was constantly coming in, so it's true to say the attack could have been called off at any time had it been deemed necessary.

Group Captain Lucking
> Yes Sir, had we realised it was a false alarm we would have called off the attack immediately.
>
> I'm afraid Sir, we were caught on the hop, it was only the third day after the declaration of war and we weren't ready.
>
> Believe me Sir, it was one hell of a wake up call for all of us, I'm sorry, mistakes happen.

Air Com Bennington
> Yes Group Captain, as you say mistakes happen but unfortunately when they result in the death of a fellow pilot some one has to be held responsible.
>
> I have no further questions.

Judge Advocate Stirling
> Sir Patrick.

Sir Patrick Hastings
> Thank you. Now group Captain you said you were surprised to see the entire 74 Squadron take off, perhaps in retrospect it might have been better had you recalled them.

Group Captain Lucking
> Yes Sir, it would but it's very easy to be wise after the event.

Sir Patrick Hastings
> Group Captain, do you accept that it was your decision not to call aircraft to return to base that directly led to the death of Pilot Officer Hulton-Hurrop.

Group Captain Lucking
> NO SIR, I DIDN'T GIVE THE ORDER TO ATTACK.

Sir Patrick Hastings
> No you didn't, but it was your decision to allow so many aircraft to take off that led to the confusion which caused the death of one of your airmen.
>
> I have no further questions for this witness.

Judge Advocate Sterling
> Air Commodore Bennington.

Air Com Bennington

Thank you, I call Squadron Leader Donaldson.

Court Usher

Squadron Leader Donaldson.

Air Com Bennington

Now you are the Squadron Leader of 151 Squadron based at North Weald.

Sqd Ldr Donaldson

Yes Sir, that is correct.

Air Com Bennington

And on the morning of 6th September I understand you were the second squadron to take off.

Sqd Ldr Donaldson

Yes Sir, I believe that is correct, we took off after 56 Squadron and climbed to our vectored height and went in search of the enemy.

There was a hell of a flap on that morning, there were aircraft from five different squadrons that had been scrambled.

Air Com Bennington

What happened later when you made contact with the enemy.

Sqd Ldr Donaldson

There was obviously a lot of confusion that morning, you have to remember it was only the third day of the war and we were all in a very heightened state of readiness, everyone was very jumpy that day.

Air Com Bennington

Yes, indeed Squadron Leader, but please just tell us what you saw when contact was made with the enemy.

Sqd Ldr Donaldson

I saw a very large group of aircraft which I assumed to be hostile until I visually confirmed that they were friendly Hurricanes.

I then saw two Spitfires turn in on two of the stragglers which I assumed to be Hurricanes and I yelled over the RT; DO NOT

RETALIATE, THEY ARE FRIENDLY, I called out three times at least, I don't know if anyone heard my transmission.

There was a Hell of a melee going on but neither of the Hurricanes fired back and in the end I saw both of them shot down, I couldn't believe it. I preyed to God they were alright, I mean they were our chaps.

I watched them go down and one didn't seem to be substantially damaged it just glided down in a left turn and hit the ground quite gently.

I later found out that that aircraft was piloted by Hulton-Hurrop who had sadly been shot and killed.

Air Com Bennington

What did you do then.

Sqd Ldr Donaldson

I was extremely angry, HOW IN GODS NAME COULD WE HAVE SHOT DOWN TWO OF OUR OWN CHAPS.

I managed to get the wing re-formed and we headed back to North Weald, I couldn't believe how our controllers had vectored two of our wings into the same air space.

Air Com Bennington

Even so, that doesn't excuse the shooting down of innocent friendly aircraft.

Sqd Ldr Donaldson

No sir, it doesn't, but I'm afraid there was utter chaos going on that morning.

Air Com Bennington

Thank you Squadron Leader Donaldson, that will be all.

Judge Advocate Sterling

Sir Patrick, do you wish to cross examine this witness.

Sir Patrick Hastings

Yes Sir, I do. Now Squadron Leader you say there was a lot of confusion that morning and it was only the third day after the declaration of war.

Sqd Ldr Donaldson

Yes Sir, that's correct.

Sir Patrick Hastings

So at this time no-one had actually come into contact with enemy aircraft.

Sqd Ldr Donaldson

Yes Sir, but we couldn't wait until we had the chance.

Sir Patrick Hastings

What precautions had been taken with regard to aircraft recognition.

Sqd Ldr Donaldson

Well Sir, we had aircraft recognition books which we used to study but it's obviously no substitute for the real thing.

Sir Patrick Hastings

Yes Squadron Leader…. no substitute for the real thing. Thank you.

Judge Advocate Sterling

Air Commodore, do you wish to re examine this witness.

Air Com Bennington

No Sir, no further questions.

Judge Advocate Sterling

Then please call your next witness.

Air Com Bennington

I call Flight Lieutenant Adolph Malan.

Court Usher

Flight Lieutenant Adolph Malan.

Air Com Bennington

Flight Lieutenant Malan, I understand you were the Flight Commander of 74 Squadron.

Flight Lt Malan

Yes Sir.

Air Com Bennington

You were leader of Red Section, 74 Squadron and were the first aircraft to take off that morning.

Flight Lt Malan

Yes Sir, I led Red Section and Yellow Section led by Flying Officer Byrne took off soon afterwards.

Air Com Bennington

Who else was in Yellow Section.

Flight Lt Malan

Pilot Officer Freeborn was flying as Yellow Two and Sergeant Pilot John Flinders was Yellow Three.

Air Com Bennington

So you took off as Red Leader with Yellow Section close behind.

Flight Lt Malan

Yes Sir, we climbed to our vectored height to the point where the enemy was supposed to be only to find it was a friendly Anson of Coastal Command.

We were pretty miffed as we were hoping it was an enemy aircraft, so we joined the two flights together and went in search of Jerry.

We caught sight of a wide Vic formation, which we thought were hostile but we were unable to get clear identification so we pressed on to attack the two aircraft which I thought were Messershmitt 109s which were flying behind and below.

Yellow Section peeled off to attack the hostile 109s and at this point I realised they were friendly and called off the attack.

Air Com Bennington

You definitely called off the attack.

Flt Lt Malan.

Yes Sir, I definitely called off the attack.

Air Com Bennington

Thank you Flight Lieutenant Malan, that will be all.

Judge Advocate Sterling

Sir Patrick.

Sir Patrick Hastings

Thank you Sir.

Now Flight Lieutenant Malan it was you who ordered the attack on the two aircraft that later turned out to be friendly.

Flight Lt Malan

Yes Sir I did, but the second I realise they were friendly I called off the attack.

Sir Patrick Hastings

Indeed, then can you explain why we could find no-one from your squadron who could confirm your alleged RT message to break off the attack.

Flight Lieutenant Malan

I don't know Sir.

Sir Patrick Hastings

I suggest to you Flight Lieutenant that the reason no-one can corroborate your testimony is because YOU ARE A BARE FACED LIAR SIR.

Flt Lieutenant Malan

NO SIR, THAT'S NOT TRUE.

Judge Advocate Sterling

It's been a long morning and we're all getting a little weary, I think that unless Air Commodore Bennington wishes to re-examine this witness, this may be a good time to adjourn for lunch.

Air Com Bennington

I have no further questions Sir.

Judge Advocate Sterling

Excellent, then this court will adjourn for lunch and re-convene in one hours time.

ADJOURN FOR LUNCH.

Air V M Callaway
>   Welcome back everyone, may I remind you that I am Air Vice
>   Marshal Callaway and I am the President of this Courts Martial.
>   I would like to say as we resume, that before luncheon some
>   remarks were passed concerning the accuracy of the evidence of
>   Flight Lieutenant Malan.
>   Whilst it may or may not be the case that Flight Lieutenant
>   Malan was not telling the truth I wish to point out to all in this
>   court that there are more gentlemanly ways to dispute evidence
>   and I suggest we stick to them.

Judge Advocate Stirling
>   Thank you Air Vice Marshal, I'm sure we all agree with you and
>   will be mindful of our language in the future.
>   I now call upon Air Commodore Bennington to call his next
>   witness.

Air Com Bennington
>   Thank you Sir, I call Pilot Officer Frank Rose.

Court Usher
>   Call Pilot Officer Frank Rose.

Air Vice Mar Callaway
>   Pilot Officer Rose, I'm Air Vice Marshal Callaway and I'm the
>   President of this Courts Martial.
>   I realise it's only six weeks since you were shot down and I just
>   wanted to check you were physically up to this cross
>   examination, we could adjourn if you're not up to it.

Pilot Officer Rose
>   Thank you sir, that's very kind of you, but I wasn't injured
>   except for a few bruises when I crash landed.

Air Vice Mar Callaway
>   I'm glad to hear that Pilot Officer Rose, you had a very lucky
>   escape.

Pilot Officer Rose
Yes Sir, very lucky, thank you.

Air Com Bennington
> Yes indeed, as the Air Vice Marshal says, a very lucky escape. Unfortunately your colleague Pilot Officer Hulton-Hurrop was not to be as lucky as you were.

Pilot Officer Rose
> Yes Sir, that's correct…I would like to say, Sir that Hurrop was one of the nicest chaps you could have wished to meet and I miss him dearly.
> It's so sad that he bought it as he did, it's an awful mess... I would like Sir, if I could to extend my condolences to his family, I only recently met them but they will be in my heart forever.

Judge Advocate Stirling
> Indeed, I'm sure everyone here today joins with you in that... please continue Air Commodore.

Air Com Bennington
> Pilot Officer Rose, can you tell the court what happened on the fateful morning of the 6th.

Pilot Officer Rose
> Well Sir, it was a Wednesday and myself and Pilot Officer Hulton-Hurrop were asleep as neither of us was on standby.
> I remember it was a Wednesday as we'd been really looking forward to a rest day for some time but we were woken by the damn bell and realised there was a flap on so we got out of bed to see what was happening, we were just expecting to see a flight take off.

Air Com Bennington
> A flight.

Pilot Officer Rose
> Yes Sir, a flight, just six aircraft.

Air Com Bennington
> And what did you see.

Pilot Officer Rose

Well Sir we stood and watched as the entire Squadron eventually take off.

Air Com Bennington

How many aircraft did you see take off.

Pilot Officer Rose

I can't be sure Sir, but the full Squadron was twenty four aircraft plus the others from 151 Squadron who shared the airfield with us.

By this time we assumed there must be a major flap on, so we joined in, we dragged our flying gear over our pyjamas and ran to our planes.

I remember shouting to Hurrop; COME ON YOU BUGGER, RUN… that's the last thing I remember saying to him.

Air Com Bennington

So you and Pilot Officer Hulton-Hurrop took off and attempted to catch up with your squadron.

Pilot Officer Rose

Yes Sir, we did, although as we had taken off later it took us longer to gain height and catch up… but we could see them in the distance.

Air Com Bennington

Then what happened.

Pilot Officer Rose

Well, I heard the RT crackle and Squadron Leader Donaldson shouting DO NOT RETALIATE, I didn't understand why, then seconds later I was being strafed by machine gun fire. I thought, MY GOD I'VE BEEN HIT, I'VE BEEN HIT…I didn't even see the bugger…I lost control of my aircraft and was plummeting towards the ground. I thought, DON'T LET IT END LIKE THIS, I'M TOO BLOODY YOUNG and I pulled with all my might on the damn stick and just managed to pull her level and belly flopped into a sugar beet field. I thought, BLIMEY THERE'LL BE HELL TO PAY FOR THIS, then I passed out.

Air Com Bennington

Yes, indeed Pilot Officer Rose and did you know what had happened to Pilot Officer Hulton-Hurrop.

Pilot Officer Rose

No Sir, at that time I was just so pleased to come to and find I was alive and that I had been able to walk away from being shot down and surviving the belly flop.

I thought I'd been shot down by the enemy, I was astounded to find out later that I'd been shot down by one of ours.

Air Com Bennington

Thank you Pilot Office Rose, as you say, shot down by one of ours... a friendly aircraft, no further questions.

Judge Advocate Sterling

Sir Patrick do you wish to cross examine this witness.

Sir Patrick Hastings

Yes Sir, I do. Pilot Officer Rose you say your Squadron was the first to be scrambled that day and that the first aircraft took off at approximately 06-27.

Pilot Officer Rose

Yes Sir.

Sir Patrick Hastings

In your previous evidence you said you watched the entire squadron take off before you put on your flying gear and chased after your squadron.

Pilot Officer Rose

Yes Sir.

Sir Patrick Hastings

Do you know how long it was after your squadron had taken off before you became airborne.

Pilot Officer Rose

I couldn't say exactly sir, but it must have been about ten or fifteen minutes.

Sir Patrick Hastings

So you were some considerable distance behind your comrades when you took off.

Pilot Officer Rose

I wouldn't say considerable, we were at full throttle and full boost, we rung those planes out to catch up.

Sir Patrick Hastings

It has been stated that you and Pilot Officer

Hulton-Hurrop were 1000 feet below and half a mile behind when you were both shot down.

Pilot Officer Rose

Yes Sir, I would say that's about right.

Sir Patrick Hastings

Did you at any time that morning consider that your actions were at all foolish.

Pilot Officer Rose

No Sir, not at all, there was an almighty flap on that day, if we'd have lost our aircraft because we left them on the ground that would have been foolish.

Sir Patrick Hastings

I'm suggesting to you that you were both shot down because you were in a place where no-one would have expected to find friendly aircraft and indeed the leading formation was totally unaware of your presence.

In fact the whole reason you and Pilot Officer Hulton-Hurrop were shot down is because you placed yourselves in a position of danger where you were both seen as hostile aircraft.

Pilot Officer Rose

NO SIR, NO SIR, that's not true.

Sir Patrick Hastings

I have no further questions for this witness.

Judge Advocate Sterling

Do you wish to examine Air Commodore Bennington.

Air Com Bennington

Yes Sir, thank you.

Pilot Officer Rose can you tell the court what the weather conditions were that morning.

Pilot Officer Rose

Well Sir I have to say it was a beautiful summer morning, a little chilly but bright and clear.

Air Com Bennington

Bright and clear, you say, a beautiful summers morning.

Pilot Officer Rose

Yes Sir.

Air Com Bennington

It's hard, is it not Pilot Officer Rose, to understand therefore how anyone could have identified you as a hostile aircraft with such good visibility.

Pilot Officer Rose

Well, yes Sir.

Air Com Bennington

I think it's also fair to say that many people will agree with your opinion about getting your aircraft airborne and to a position of safety, but I think they will also agree that there can never be an excuse for shooting down a friendly aircraft whatever the circumstances.

Pilot Officer Rose

Yes Sir, no excuse.

Air Com Bennington

No further questions.

Judge Advocate Sterling

Then please call your next witness Sir Patrick.

Sir Patrick Hastings

I call Flying Officer Vincent Byrne.

Court Usher

Call Flying Officer Vincent Byrne.

Sir Patrick Hastings

Flying Officer Byrne, you were Yellow Leader on the morning of 6th September.

Flying Officer Byrne

Yes Sir.

Sir Patrick Hastings

We've heard of the events of that morning from other witnesses, can we hear your version.

Flying Officer Byrne

Well Sir, briefly it's simple, we took off and joined Red Section of 74 Squadron, we went looking for the enemy and found what we thought to be enemy aircraft.

There were two stragglers which we were ordered to attack which we did.

At no time during the attack did we have reason to question the order to attack nor did we receive any order to break off the attack.

It was sheer bad luck that the aircraft we attacked turned out to be friendly, GOD KNOWS I WISH IT WERE NOT TRUE, BUT IT WAS SHEER BAD LUCK, SIR.

Sir Patrick Hastings

You say you had no reason to question the order to attack.

Flying Officer Byrne

Yes Sir, we had no reason to question the order and if we had disobeyed there would have been Hell to pay.

We had no option we had to attack, had we not done so we would have been on a charge of insubordination.

Sir Patrick Hastings

Just to reiterate, at no time did you hear an order to call off the attack.

Flying Officer Byrne

Yes Sir, that's correct.

Sir Patrick Hastings
> Thank you Flying Officer, no further questions.

Judge Advocate Sterling
> Air Commodore Bennington do you wish to question this witness.

Air Com Bennington
> Yes Sir I do. Flying Officer Byrne you said in your evidence you didn't hear any order to break off the attack.

Flying Officer Byrne
> Yes Sir that's correct.

Air Com Bennington
> Might I suggest to you Flying Officer that just because you didn't hear an RT message to break off doesn't mean one wasn't sent, there are any number of reasons why you may not have heard the message.
>
> In the heat of what had now become battle perhaps your concentration was too fixed on the attack for you to notice.

Flying Officer Byrne
> No Sir, if anything your senses become more heightened in a combat situation.

Air Com Bennington
> Could it be that you switched radio channels during the attack.

Flying Officer Byrne
> No Sir, we wouldn't have done that we were too focused on the attack.

Air Com Bennington
> Too focused on the attack Flying Officer Byrne.
> No further questions.

Judge Advocate Sterling
> Sir Patrick do you wish to re-examine.

Sir Patrick Hastings
> Yes Sir.

Flying Officer Byrne you just stated that your senses become more acute in a combat situation and that it is unlikely that you would have changed radio frequency during the battle.

You were all sufficiently alert to hear the order to attack, can you think of any other reason why you wouldn't have heard the message to break off.

Flying Officer Byrne
Yes Sir, no message was sent.

Sir Patrick Hastings
Thank you, no further questions.

Judge Advocate Sterling
Do you wish to call any further witnesses Sir Patrick.

Sir Patrick Hastings
Yes Sir I call my last witness Pilot Office John Freeborn.

Court Usher
Pilot Officer John Freeborn.

Sir Patrick Hastings
Pilot Officer Freeborn, on the morning of the 6th you were flying as Yellow Two of 74 Squadron.

Pilot Officer Freeborn
Yes Sir I took off behind Flying Officer Byrne who was Yellow Leader.

Sir Patrick Hastings
Please tell the court what happened up to the point where the unfortunate Hulton-Hurrop was shot down and killed.

Pilot Officer Freeborn
Well Sir, we took off slightly behind Red Section as we had to wait for Paddy, that's Flying Officer Byrne to clear an engine misfire. We chased after Red Section to our vectored height and location only to find a friendly Anson of Coastal Command.
We stayed in a tight formation then suddenly we spotted the enemy and Flight Lieutenant Malan came over the RT shouting

TALLY HO, NUMBER ONE, ATTACK GO.

There was a hell of a lot of chaos going on , but we realised the aircraft we'd gone after were friendly so went after the two planes that were shadowing the main formation believing them to be hostile Messershmitt 109s. Flying Officer Byrne took one and I took the other, I fired a short burst and was surprised to see the aircraft plummet to the earth.

I never thought it would be that easy to shoot an aircraft down, but was obviously elated to have made my first kill of the war.

Sir Patrick Hastings

And then you flew back to base.

Pilot Officer Freeborn

Yes Sir, when I landed back at Hornchurch I could hear Sammy Samson our CO shouting, WHERE THE HELL IS MALAN, I WANT HIM HERE NOW.

But he'd done his usual bunk and gone home to his wife who was billeted off the airfield.

Myself and Flying Officer Bryne were both placed under close arrest and I was devastated when I was told the Messershmitt had in fact been a friendly aircraft.

We were both debriefed by the CO and that's all I can tell you Sir.

Sir Patrick Hastings

Thank you Pilot Officer Freeborn, I have just two further questions for you. Firstly can you confirm that you heard Flight Lieutenant Malan give the command Tally Ho, Number One, Attack Go.

Pilot Officer Freeborn

Yes Sir, everyone heard it.

Sir Patrick Hastings

And my second question for you, Pilot Officer is that at no time did you received the RT message to break off the attack.

Pilot Officer Freeborn

Yes Sir, at no time did we get the call to break off.

Sir Patrick Hastings
Thank you, no further questions.

Judge Advocate Sterling
Air Commodore Bennington.

Air Com Bennington
Thank you Sir.
I only have one question for this witness and that is , are you sure, and think carefully before you answer, are you sure that at no time you heard a RT message to break off the attack.

Pilot Officer Freeborn
Sir, I can tell you quite categorically that I have never before in my life been in a situation where I was so aware of my feelings.
My entire body was alive to a point I had no idea it could reach, my senses were so heightened I could have heard a pin drop in the cockpit let alone an RT message.

That's what combat is like Sir.

Judge Advocate Sterling
I assume that's all the questions you have for this witness Air Commodore.

Air Com Bennington
Yes Sir.

Judge Advocate Sterling
We have heard all the evidence and I now call upon Air Commodore Bennington to make his closing address.

Air Com Bennington
Thank you Sir.
The tragic death of Pilot officer Hulton-Hurrop I believe, could have been avoided.
Were it not for the actions of Flying Officer Byrne and specifically Pilot Officer Freeborn, both young and inexperienced airmen I believe this tragedy would have been averted.
It is my contention that the irresponsible and gung ho actions of Pilot Officer Freeborn in particular caused the death of Pilot Officer Hulton-Hurrop.

Whether or not you believe they were given the order to break off the attack, there can be no excuse for shooting down a friendly aircraft and for this reason alone I ask this court to find Pilot Officer Freeborn guilty.

Judge Advocate Sterling

Thank you Air Commodore, I now call upon Sir Patrick Hastings for his closing statement for the defence.

Sir Patrick Hastings

Thank you sir.

Young, inexperienced, yes they were, but all the airmen that day were young and inexperienced, it

was the third day of the war, no one had any experience of combat.

The whole day was peppered with unfortunate errors from the moment it started with the take off of so many aircraft; aircraft that could and perhaps should have been recalled.

The foolhardy but none the less understandable actions of Pilot Officer Hulton-Hurrop and Pilot Officer Rose in chasing after their Squadron which led to them being identified as hostile aircraft.

The vectoring of two Wings of aircraft into the same air space was also a contributory factor which led to the order to attack being given.

Lastly and most importantly we could find no one who heard the order to break off the attack. The weight of evidence we believe gives this court no option but to find Pilot Officer Freeborn not guilty.

Judge Advocate Sterling

Thank you Sir Patrick. I would now ask that the court be cleared while Air Vice Marshal Callaway and the other members of this Courts Martial come to their decision.

Court Usher

Court rise.

THE COURT EMPTIES

EVERYONE RETURNS TO THE COURTROOM.

Judge Advocate Sterling

> Thank you for your patience everyone, Air Vice Marshal
> Callaway have you reached a verdict.

Air V M Callaway

> Yes Sir we have, but before we give our decision we would like
> on behalf of this court to offer our condolences to Pilot Officer
> Hulton-Hurrops parents and family.
>
> This whole incident was full of unfortunate errors right from the
> start.
>
> Criticism can be levelled at the decision to allow too many
> aircraft to take off and the decision to vector two Wings into the
> same air space.
>
> We view the actions of Pilot Officer Hulton-Hurrop and Pilot
> Officer Rose in taking off to follow their Squadron as foolish,
> but who here amongst us would not have done the same.
>
> Now to the evidence, and we feel the most crucial evidence of
> this Courts Martial, that of Flight Lieutenant Malan who ordered
> the attack on the unfortunate Pilot Officer Hulton-Hurrop.
>
> We would criticise whole heartedly the evidence of this officer,
> the decision to attack was his and his alone and perhaps one
> made in haste, but under the circumstances understandable.
>
> What is not understandable and is the crucial point of this case is
> his evidence about the RT message to break off the attack.
>
> We believe that at no time was that message sent and we
> therefore find Pilot Officer John Freeborn, not guilty.

BUS STOP.

CHARACTER BREAKDOWN

DONALD PLANT, WHITE, MIDDLE CLASS, 60, SEMI RETIRED.

JOHN COLEMAN, WHITE, WORKING CLASS, 50, UNEMPLOYED.

JACQUELINE AOLA, BLACK, MIDDLE CLASS, 29, LAWYER.

ALL THE ACTION TAKES PLACE AT A BUS STOP.

JOHN IS SEATED AT THE BUS STOP AND DONALD
ENTERS STAGE LEFT.

DONALD

Excuse me, am I right in thinking I can get a bus here to get to
Stanstead.

JOHN

Yeah you can but God knows how long you'll have to wait, I've
been here bleeding ages and nothing's come by at all.

DONALD

Oh dear, that's a shame I've just dropped my classic car at the
garage and was hoping to get to Stanstead to catch the train back
to London.

JOHN

What's your car.

DONALD

A 1939 Rover 12.

JOHN

Sounds nice must be worth a few bob.

DONALD

Well not a fortune, about eleven thousand.

JOHN

That's a fortune to me.

DONALD

Yes, I suppose so, it's my pride and joy.

JOHN

Those were the days, 1939, no bleeding foreigners here then.

DONALD

I think you'll find there were, this country is built on foreign
invasion. The Saxons from Germany, the Normans from
France, the Vikings from Scandinavia, the Romans from Italy,
the Jews, the Irish, the West Indians, the…

JOHN

All right, all right, I didn't want a bleeding history lesson.

DONALD

Sorry, I was just…

JOHN

Bleeding typical.

DONALD

Sorry.

JOHN

Bleeding typical, no bus, I bet the drivers a bloody Pole, probably can't read and got lost.

DONALD

I doubt it.

JOHN

What do you mean, I doubt it.

DONALD

Well, the fact that no traffic has passed would suggest there must have been an accident and the police have a diversion in place.

JOHN

Yeah, well I bet some bloody foreigner caused it, none of them can drive, especially the Pakis and the Yids.

DONALD

I don't think that's true there are bad drivers of all races and sexes.

JOHN

You've got an answer for everything, haven't you, I bet you think women can drive.

DONALD

Of course they can statistically they're safer than men.

JOHN

What's your name mate.

DONALD

Donald, and you.

JOHN

John, it's John, a good old fashioned British name. Donald I think you're talking a load of bollocks.

DONALD

I'm afraid it's true, that's why women get cheaper car insurance.

JOHN

Bloody women, bloody foreigners, this country is going to the dogs, I blame the government.

DONALD

Well John, we only get the government we elect, if you don't like them don't vote for them.

JOHN

Listen mate, I don't vote for any of them any more.

DONALD

Then I would suggest you don't have the right to complain.

JOHN

Yes I do, this is my bloody country, the government should be looking after me not these foreign dole scroungers. I read the Daily Mail mate there's always some story of these scrounging bastards.

DONALD

Well John, I don't believe those stories they only get what they are entitled to, we are in the European Union now. I'm sure the vast majority of immigrants to this country are honest and hard working.

JOHN

Yeah too bleeding hard working, coming over here undercutting us, putting people like me out of work.

31

DONALD

That's a shame, but it's not their fault, it's modern life, supply and demand. It's a very competitive world in which we live, we're all being undercut, I blame Margret Thatcher, she started it, she broke the unions and we've been paying the price ever since.

JOHN

How can you say that Donald, those were the best years of my life I had loads of money and Thatcher made it happen for us, I wish she was still in power, I'd vote for her again. I had my own building business; I made a bloody fortune, no foreigners undercutting us then.

DONALD

I bet you lost it all.

JOHN

What.

DONALD

All the money, I bet you lost it.

JOHN

How'd you know that.

DONALD

It's not rocket science, it's human nature; greed, it's always greed with any financial bubble. It amazes me the number of people you meet who lost everything and still say they'd vote for Thatcher again, personally I hate her.

JOHN

Surely you vote Conservative.

DONALD

You've got to be joking after what Thatcher did to the country I couldn't vote for them ever. That damn woman took all the oil revenue and wasted it giving us all tax breaks and she let our industry go to the wall. I'm old enough to remember when you didn't see foreign cars in this country, British products were the best in the world, then with no investment they became some of the worst; have you ever driven a Morris Marina. We used to have a fabulous manufacturing industry in this country, coal mining, ship building, car manufacture, the motorcycle industry, she let them all go to the dogs and she had the money to save them.

JOHN

Perhaps you're right, but I'd still have her back; that was the richest I've ever been

DONALD

I think you have a strange outlook on life, especially your xenophobia.

JOHN

My what.

DONALD

Your hatred of foreigners.

JOHN

Oh yeah, very clever, you're a right smart arse you are.

DONALD

Can I ask you a question.

JOHN

I can't stop you.

DONALD

Do you watch football.

JOHN

Yeah all the time, I love it.

DONALD

I must say I don't, but I know a little about it and I was told that Arsenal only have one English player so how does that fit with your views.

JOHN

That's different, their not over here scrounging.

DONALD

So it's scroungers you dislike, not foreigners.

JOHN

No, you're twisting my words, I hate foreigners.

DONALD

Obviously not all of them, or is it just the ones who can't play football.

JOHN

I've had enough of this, you've made my head ache.

DONALD

Sorry, I was just trying to stand up for the under dog, so to speak. Oh look, some ones coming.

JACUELINE ENTERS STAGE LEFT.

JACQUELINE

Can I join you I need a sit down, my feet are killing me, these shoes aren't made for walking.

JOHN

What's going on down the road.

JACQUELINE

There's been an accident it's blocked the road, luckily no one was hurt but they won't let any one through.

JOHN

How'd you get through then.

JACQUELINE

I used my feminine charm, that and the fact that I'm a barrister and have to get to my next trial at Stanstead Crown Court this afternoon.

JOHN

Bloody typical the law always sticks together.

JACQUELINE

I don't think that's true, still never mind, how far is it to Stanstead from here.

JOHN
> You've no chance of walking there by the afternoon, if I was you I'd sit on this bench rest your plates and watch the world go by.

JACQUELINE
> ON THE PHONE
> Hello, Clerk of the Courts office please….Hello, yes I'm Jacqueline Aola I'm supposed to be with you this afternoon, Crown versus Coleman, I'm afraid I've been held up in an accident and may not be with you in time. If I can get through I will phone to let you know….Ok, thanks bye.

JOHN
> Did you say Crown versus Coleman.

JACQUELINE
> Yes, but it's sub judice for me to discuss the case with you.

JOHN
> Not if my names John Coleman.

JACQUELINE
> John Coleman of 27 Denby Road.

JOHN
> Yeah, that's me. So like I said just sit down and rest your plates, because I'm not going to kill myself getting to court.

JACQUELINE
> Perhaps we'd better discuss the brief just in case we get through, I always believe in being as well prepared as possible.

JOHN
> Ok if you insist.

JACQUELINE
> All right John, you've been charged with assult on William Eddington the BNP candidate for Stanstead. It seems he was making a speech in the High Road when you made an unprovoked attack on him.

35

JOHN

That's not true; he was holding a meeting and he called my wife a nigger and I threw a can of Coke at him.

DONALD

Why on earth did he call your wife a nigger, I thought you hated scrounging foreigners.

JOHN

Why do you think.

DONALD

Your wife's black.

JOHN

Yeah, but she's not a scrounging foreigner she was born here she's British.

JACQUELINE

Unfortunately in law that's not an excuse for assult.

DONALD

Suppose we found a witness who could state that John didn't throw the can.

JACQUELINE

Well there's no CCTV so it's your word against his.

DONALD

I think we may be able to do that, I'm sure now that I think about it I was standing behind John on…

JOHN

23rd July.

DONALD

Yes, on the 23rd at about…

JOHN

2-45

DONALD

That's right it was 2-45 on the 23rd July and I would swear that at no time did John throw anything.

JACQUELINE

Are you aware of the law concerning perjury.

DONALD

I am and I'm sure William Eddington and his BNP are aware too but with no CCTV it will be our word against his, I think we have him outnumbered.

JACQUELINE

Well if we are going to take him on we'd better get a move on there must be somewhere up the road to get a taxi.

JACQUELINE STARTS TO EXIT STAGE RIGHT.

DONALD

Ok lets go.

JOHN

Donald, thanks, but why.

DONALD

I told you earlier, we only get the government we vote for unless we can discredit them before they get a chance to be elected.

JACQUELINE

Come on you two.

THEY ALL EXIT STAGE RIGHT.

HI DIDDLE DEE DEE.

Hi Diddle Dee Dee is set in the dressing rooms of ten of the cast in
the pantomime Cinderella. The story is about the relationship between
all of them and how they may not be quite as they are seen.

CHARACTER BREAKDOWN

ERIC SHIRVELL, 45 GAY/VERY CAMP, BACK END OF PANTO HORSE.

GEORGE DAVIES, 50 JOBBING ACTOR, FRONT END OF PANTO HORSE.

TRACY PHILLIPS, 21 FRESH FROM DRAMA SCHOOL, CINDERELLA.

JOHN SYNDON, 30 YOUNG SOAP ACTOR, PRINCE CHARMING.

GWEN THOMAS, 65 OLD SOAP ACTOR, FAIRY GODMOTHER.

ROSIE MORTON, 48 SEX MAD JOBBING ACTOR, DANDINI.

DONALD COLEPEPPER, OLD STYLE RSC ACTOR, BARON HARDUP.

WAYNE PETERS, 65 OLD 60's POP STAR, BUTTONS.

BERT BAXTER, 65 OLD STYLE COMEDIAN, UGLY SISTER.

NORMAN ALLEN, 65 OLD STYLE COMEDIAN, GAY, UGLY SISTER.

SCENE ONE. THE FIRST NIGHT.

THE DRESSING ROOM
DOOR OPENS

ERIC

George you're such a bloody liar.

GEORGE

I don't know what you mean.

ERIC

Yes you do you bastard, get me out of this, the bloody zip is stuck again.

GEORGE

There, better now Eric.

ERIC

No, look George you said no more rubies when we're working and you farted constantly.

GEORGE

Don't be such an old queen.

ERIC

It's all right for you, you bastard, you're in the front, you should try mincing about stuck in here with your head up some ones arse.

GEORGE

All right Erica dear, calm down, I'm sorry for farting.

ERIC

It's not just the farting, although God knows it's driving me mad. One night we ought to swap ends and see how you like it.

GEORGE

Not with my back I can't, you know how I suffer with my back, I'm in constant pain, I've tried everything.

ERIC

Perhaps you ought to have a word with Rosie, I've heard she does that massage where they walk on your back, very therapeutic so I'm told by Mike in the band.

GEORGE

Well even if you fix it, I'm still not going in the back.

ERIC

I'd like to get Trevor in the back of this thing when you're having one of your bad nights.

GEORGE

Our esteemed director, well yes I'm inclined to agree with you, God knows how he became a director.

ERIC

Like an awful lot of them deary, he's a failed actor, I've met so many of them in my time. It's all just a power trip for them. The only reason he's doing this is he can't get anything better; he's not fit to direct traffic.

GEORGE

He's not that bad, he could manage traffic, just about.

ERIC

How can it have come to this, I went to RADA for Gods sake. My best friend then was Laurence Booth, look how successful he has been since leaving. He's been playing Pontius Pilate in Joseph for years, that's where I should be, not the back end of a pantomime horse in Cleethorpes.

GEORGE

The trouble is that's all he's done since leaving RADA, low budget films and the tour of Joseph, over and over again, it would have driven you mad. Anyway what do you mean RADA, they chucked you out after the first term.

ERIC

That's not the point, I've served my time, I've done years of training, look at my CV, what have this lot done of any worth.

Look at Tracy, Miss Thing, Phillips, straight out of University with a Performing Arts Degree. How did she get Cinderella, don't make me play the who's sleeping with the director game dear.

GEORGE

Well every ones got to start somewhere.

ERIC

I know George, I've just had enough, I'm sick to death of it. Flogging myself to death eight shows a week for Equity minimum in some God forsaken place, what's the point.

GEORGE

Money, that's the point, if you had my ex wife to pay you'd see the point, I have to pay for her and the kids every week regardless of whether I'm working or not, it drives me mad. I know she's got another bloke, but until he moves in, they're just good friends and so I keep having to pay. I think I'll join Fathers for Justice, how do you fancy climbing on the roof of the House of Commons with me in the horse suit and Superman on our back.

ERIC

Are you mad I hate heights.

GEORGE

I didn't expect the answer to be yes, by the way, but it would be a bit of fun. That's the trouble I'm stuck working any show I can get just like you, what else can we do, you're not exactly cut out to be a bricklayer and think how quickly you'd be bored to death flouncing about in a hairdressers making tea.

ERIC

It's all right for you, you don't care what you do as long as you're working.

GEORGE

Oh, don't I. I'll have you know I care very much, even now. I still live in hopes of that big break, I did Chekhov last year.

ERIC

At Edinburgh in a grotty church hall.

GEORGE

Better than never at all and it wasn't in a church hall, it was in the Traverse Theatre; we had full houses all through the run and some of the best revues I've ever had. That's what made it worth it; it's not about the money.

ERIC

I admire your perseverance George I really do, but I've just run out of energy. I hate this bloody company, look at them. Buttons. Buttons, have you ever met anyone so arrogant. Ex pop star Wayne Peters, if he could stick to the script we could get home half an hour earlier every night. Have you any idea how old he is.

GEORGE

He says he's forty nine.

ERIC

Don't make me laugh dear, if he's forty nine that would make us about sixty.

GEORGE

Well he is the housewives favourite and he puts bums on seats.

ERIC

He may be the housewives favourite but he isn't anybody else's favourite. I know when he was doing Singing in the rain, everyone, even front of house used to piss in the tank they used for the rain. That's how popular he was dear.

GEORGE

Well no one's perfect.

ERIC

Yes, they also pissed in the bath when he did Some like it hot, just ask Dilly the SM.

GEORGE

I've never quite got along with her, she seems such an aggressive old dyke.

ERIC

No she isn't, it's just a front, a defence.

GEORGE

I know I shouldn't say it, but it's the tattoos, they look like they were done with a rusty nail. The sad thing is I know underneath she's a really attractive girl.

ERIC

She is, in fact she's one of the few people on this job that I can actually have a conversation with. You know her girlfriend is Sarah; yeah stunning Sarah, could have been a model Sarah, like they say, never judge a book by its cover.

GEORGE

Things aren't that bad then that's Dilly and Fairy Godmother that you like.

ERIC

Gwen Thomas soap star, well she makes me laugh, though probably not for the right reasons. I'm sure she means well, but when she's on she's fumbling with her lines and the rest of the time she's off having a fag at the stage door. It's not fair George, look how long we were left hoofing last night before she realised it was her cue. I was bloody knackered, my lallies were killing me. Then on she strolls in a world of her own and utters the wrong line.

GEORGE

Come on Erica love, I've never seen you like this before, cheer up.

ERIC

Cheer up, cheer up, are you mad. We're working with Bert Baxter the most homophobic comic since Kenny Lanning and you want me to cheer up. Ugly Sister, yes, ugly is an understatement and I don't just mean his eek. I wouldn't trust him as far as I could throw him. I was up for a commercial a few years ago and so was he, but he went in first. When I went in the director asked me if I was feeling better. I told him I was; well I'd just had my piles done. I didn't get the job, nor did I ever work for that director again. It was years later I found out he'd told them I had aids.

GEORGE

Well I'd like to say I'm surprised, but sadly I'm not.

ERIC

Here's one if you want to be surprised, Simon.

GEORGE

What Simon the MD.

ERIC

Yes, Simon, nice as pie, friend to all, Simon.

GEORGE

So, what, tell me.

ERIC

He's in the BNP dear, he's a narrow minded bigot he hates me and Dilly; he's probably in the Bert Baxter fan club dear. That's why he never speaks to anyone.

GEORGE

I just thought he was a muso who just wanted to be in the pub with the rest of the band getting pissed.

ERIC

Sometimes you're delightfully naive George it's Simon who fixes the band, they are all in it together and even if they're not no one is going to say anything, they can be replaced just like that.

GEORGE

Well what about the other sister Norman Allen he's not like that, he's a well respected family man isn't he, I know there were rumours a few years ago.

ERIC

Rumours, rumours dear, I should say so; he's a naff old queen and a bitchy one too. Have you ever seen his wife, they haven't lived together for years it's all just a front. Just follow him one night when he's off cottaging and as for the rug dear, it looks more like a door mat.

GEORGE

Well I'm no oil painting.

ERIC

That's different, you're my friend.

GEORGE

Thanks Eric that means a lot to me.

ERIC

Well it's the little things that make the difference don't they George. I remember the time that bitch Allison from front of house said we'd all got to do the publicity photos outside on the front and it was bloody snowing and you stood up to her and said no.

GEORGE

Well I had to I'm the Equity dep.

ERIC

It was still very brave of you, I mean I'll stand up for myself but she's a very scary woman, there's something just not right about her. She's always hanging around with those odd looking blokes; they look like ex KGB.

GEORGE

I know what you mean, I'm sure she's dealing drugs; she certainly hangs around with some very dubious looking characters.

ERIC

I'm sorry George it must be my time of the month but things just seem to be getting on top of me at the moment. Mind you the only one who hasn't got on top of me is Rosie Morton. I mean that literally, I think she thinks she can change me, God knows why. I keep telling her I'm an omi-palone, gay dear, homosexual, will she listen. No. I'm Dandini she says, I'm a man too. Sad old cow she'd shag anything with a pulse.

GEORGE

I don't think that's true, not anything.

47

ERIC

Oh George, I'm sorry I didn't mean you.

GEORGE

It's alright Eric dear, I was feeling a bit lonely.

ERIC

I know what you mean, you do some silly things when you're feeling lonely. I've been having a bit of a thing with Camp David.

GEORGE

You mean young David in the chorus.

ERIC

Yes, that David. The thing is he's not even gay, I know he thinks he is at the moment but just wait until this is over and he wouldn't give me a second glance. That's the way it is, I'm desperate and he's lonely.

GEORGE

Yes, we all need someone who cares, especially when we're on tour.

ERIC

That's half the problem, feeling lonely, it's hard not to when you've only this lot to choose from. Look at Baron Hardup, poor old git; I'm Donald Colepepper I've been with the RSC for years. Yes dear, you have, but you're not there any more, those days are gone. I'm sick to death of his stories of when I was at the National with Johnny and Ralphy.

GEORGE

Perhaps you're right, but we can't give in we've a show to finish.

ERIC

Show to finish, are you mad. I'm on the verge of suicide and you're talking about finishing the show.

GEORGE

Come on, the second acts very short and it is our big number with Prince Charming.

ERIC

Yes it is our big number but can you remember how hard we had to work for that number, I nearly left the show because of it. Bloody Sophie Augins, she's a bitch.

GEORGE

Surely she's just a perfectionist.

ERIC

No George, she's a bitch; I've known her since the beginning when I met her in Pineapple. I used to go to the same cattle call auditions that she went to. Hundreds of dancers in the day all fighting to be one of ten or twenty for some minor pop video or trade show. She was a hard faced cow even then. Pity anyone trying to pick up the routine should ask her for the counts. It's not that hard to tell them; no it's five six seven eight and one two and three and four, I mean how hard is that. It's easy, if you help them and they get the job it just means they've got the look they were after. You know in those days all they wanted was white girls with blond hair. She was the first to have her hair dyed although she swore it was natural, but I know girls who saw her in the shower and she didn't have a matching set. Then she made it in one of those dance groups on Top of the pops, Hot Sex, or whatever they were called. She was a pushy cow, don't get me wrong I admire her success in a way, but I think she paid a high price for it. She lost her soul. Then eventually she got too old to dance and became a choreographer and destroyed the lives of so many girls who joined the group. So many of them got anorexia or became addicted to drugs to keep their weight down. She was a cow; she didn't care as long as the show looked good. Now she's taking it out on us.

GEORGE

I'm sure you're right, but we still have our big number with Prince Charming.

ERIC

How in Hells name you can call John Sydon charming is beyond belief. I'm sure he's a paedophile, have you seen him with the young kids in the chorus. Most of the time he's so coked up he's almost incoherent. It's all too depressing I think I'm going to cry.

GEORGE

Oh Eric, I hate to see you cry; John isn't that bad, you're just having a bad day. Let me give you a hug; you know the show must go on.

ERIC

Must it George, must it.

STAGE MANAGER

Act two beginners this is your call.

GEORGE

Yes Erica dear, it must. Now wipe your eyes, it's show time.

ERIC

Thanks George, of course you're right. There's just one thing.

GEORGE

What's that.

ERIC

Just promise you won't fart second act.

GEORGE

All right, I promise.

THE DOOR OPENS AND
PLAYING IN THE
BACKGROUND WE HEAR
THE OVERTURE.

SCENE TWO. THE SECOND NIGHT.

A KNOCK AT THE DOOR

JOHN

Tracy, its John.

TRACY

Come in.

JOHN

Hiya, you're in early tonight.

TRACY

Yeah, I came in to run through a couple of new numbers with Simon.

JOHN

New numbers, just for you.

TRACY

Yes, it was Trevor's idea.

JOHN

Oh, Trevor's idea eh, has he any other plans for anyone else, do you know.

TRACY

Not as far as I know, why is that a problem.

JOHN

No, not at all, it's nice to see someone young who's enthusiastic about their career. I'm afraid I've become a bit lax with mine. It's sad, I'm not that much older than you and yet we're so far apart. I can remember being like you, a fresh faced youth just out of drama school and desperate to succeed. It's surprising how soon you learn to compromise, to settle for second best.

TRACY

What on earth are you talking about, you're in Eastsiders, you're famous. I see your face in the magazines every week; you're always at some party or other. You're rich, you're successful, what more can you want.

JOHN

Yeah, but look who's at those parties; sad C list celebrities desperate for some publicity. I don't want to be there, I want what you've got, I want to be back at the very start of my career, I want to start again.

TRACY

What on earth for, you've made it.

JOHN

Made it, is that what you think Tracy.

TRACY

Yes, that is what I think, you're in one of the most successful soaps on tele, you earn a fortune and you want more. For what it's worth I think you're a greedy bastard, most of us would give our right arm for what you've got, you should be so grateful for what you have.

JOHN

I am grateful, I am, I can't tell you how grateful I am. In many ways I have everything I could ask for, I've shed loads of money, I'm famous, for what that's worth, I can have any girl I want, I should be as happy as a pig in shit. The trouble is in real life I'm still like you. I was bloody lucky getting Eastsiders so early, I thought at the time, I've hit the big time what more can I want. It's only now I'm beginning to know what I really want.

TRACY

I'm sorry but from where I'm seeing this you still seem to be somewhat ungrateful to say the least.

JOHN

I can see why you think like that, but don't believe all you read in the tabloid press. I'm not a coke addict, never was. I have a speech impediment which comes on when I'm stressed or tired which makes me slur my speech. Ok I used to do a line every now and then but never anything serious. The trouble is once the press have an opinion on you that's what sticks and people believe it. All that rubbish about being at so and so's party and all the other things, so much of it isn't true. You know there was a rumour I was a paedophile, just because I liked being with the young kids. There's a reason I like being with the young people, it reminds me of my sister Holly who died when she was eleven. She had melingitis and I miss her like hell. That's why I like being with young people, it reminds me of the good days with my sister.

We used to have such good times, I was her elder brother, I should have been there to look after her. It was because of her I'm in the business; I went with my mother when she took Holly to ballet class and I wanted to join in, that was the start of my career. I wish she was here today to share my success, well not all of it, not the silly parties. People like me go to the opening of an envelope just to keep our faces in the press, because without the publicity we're dead. Do you remember when you started your career, doing some fringe play in a pub theatre, or some low budget film about some worthy topic. That's where I started, a fringe play about The Marchioness River Boat disaster, a play that eventually made a difference to safety on the Thames river boats. That's where I want to be, I want to be

doing something that matters, not leaning on the bar in The Red Lion in Eastsiders asking for a pint and chatting about the weather. I don't want to be a Gwen Thomas, God knows she means well but look at the poor old cow. She's been in Grange Road since the first episode, you know the one they keep showing on the outtake shows, the one where the set fell down. Nothing much has changed there, the sets still wobble and so do the actors. I know they joke that they wheel Gwen about on a dolly but I don't think it's far from the truth.

TRACY

I think she's sweet.

JOHN

She is but I can't stand to see her, she's me in thirty or forty years time if I don't do something about my situation. The only reason she's still in Grange Road is to pay for her scrounging children.

TRACY

You have a very jaded outlook on life, I'm surprised, you're nothing like I thought you were.

JOHN

I know, I'm sorry, I told you I'm not like my tabloid persona.

TRACY

I didn't mean that, I meant you seem a bit sad.

JOHN

I am bloody sad, you're right; I'm drowning in a sea of success. That's the problem with the press; all you ever see is me going to parties apparently enjoying myself, when I'm actually a far more serious person who's desperately concerned about his career.

TRACY

Why don't you just ask them for better story lines.

JOHN

You have no idea how many times I've asked, I even slept with one of the producers in the hope it would make a difference. I know it's mad but I want to be like Donald Colepepper.

TRACY

He's a boring old fart.

JOHN

He may be to you and to some of the others, but if you really listen to what he has to say you can really learn from him. Have you ever bothered to look him up in Spotlight and read his CV, he's done everything that's worth doing and more.

TRACY

The trouble is he rabbits on about the old days all the time, that's why no one listens to him.

JOHN

Well perhaps you should listen in the future, he taught me loads of things and he's some great stories about the old days. Do you know the one where he was in rehearsals with Johnny Gielgud and Johnny came up to him and asked him; what are you doing in this scene Donald. Donald had no lines in the scene and said to Johnny I'm doing nothing in this scene, whereupon Johnny turned to Donald and said; oh no, you can't be doing nothing in this scene dear boy; I'm doing nothing in this scene. That's class, I love it.

TRACY

Yeah, but he's skint and he's doing this for the money and you're doing it for the publicity.

JOHN

What about the other one he tells about Dustin Hoffman when he was working with Laurence Olivier in Marathon Man. Dustin has to run into the room out of breath as it's a cut from outside when he was jogging. So before the director calls action Dustin starts running up and down the studio, the director calls action and into the room runs the out of breath Hoffman. They do endless takes as they do in film, Hoffman the method actor keeps running before every take. Finally the director is satisfied with the shot and Olivier says to the exhausted Hoffman; have you ever thought of trying acting dear boy. You've got to admit he had a point, I'm a great believer in method acting but you can take it too far sometimes. You know in some ways I'd rather be like George.

TRACY

I see what you're saying about starting again, but surely you don't want to be like George, although at least he's the front of the horse.

JOHN

I do, that's my point, he did Chekhov last year at Edinburgh.

TRACY

For peanuts though.

JOHN

It's not about the money, it's about the quality of the work.

TRACY

That's easy for you to say, you're rich, you could do something like that any time you want.

JOHN

No, that's where you're wrong, if I leave Eastsiders and I'm off the tele for six months I'm as good as dead. How many times have you heard people say, whatever happened to so and so, I thought he was dead.

TRACY

I know what you're saying but you have the money which gives you the opportunity to take a chance, to do something risky.

JOHN

Ok, Tracy, I give in you're right, I'll tell you the truth. I'd love to do Chekhov or something risky. You know what stops me, I'm scared to death of failure. I can stand in the bar in Eastsiders and do my lines week in week out, it's safe, it's within my comfort zone. Can you imagine the reviews if I did Chekhov and made a mess of it, they'd slaughter me. Then see how quickly my storylines in Siders would dry up and my character would have a nasty accident or leave to go on the run in Spain to escape from some minor gangster.

TRACY

That's really sad John, I thought you'd made it, I thought you had everything you could possibly want; now you've depressed me. I can't tell you how pleased I was when I got this job; it's my first since leaving Uni. I fought hard to get it; I had three recalls before they finally told me I'd got it. I nearly wet myself I was so excited, I beat four other girls to get this job fair and square.

JOHN

I don't want to upset you but the rumour going round is that you only got it because you slept with the director.

TRACY

Slept with Trevor, are you mad, who told you that.

JOHN

Oh, no one.

TRACY

That's terrible, Trevor and I are good friends he went to school

56

with my cousin, but we're certainly not sleeping together. He's a lovely bloke to talk to but sexually I wouldn't fancy him if he was the last man in the world. I hate beer guts, no no no, not Trevor.

JOHN

I'm sorry I got it wrong, it's so easy to believe the rumours.

TRACY

It's the same with the rumour about Eric being a bitchy old queen. He certainly isn't like that with me; he's been the most helpful member of the company as far as I'm concerned. I remember when I first arrived I bumped into him at the train station, we shared a cab as his digs were close to mine. He came round later to see how I'd settled in and found me in floods of tears; my digs were absolutely awful, there was mould and damp everywhere. He physically dragged me out and told the landlord where to stick his agreement. Five minutes later I was in a cab with Eric on the phone and ten minutes later I was at the new digs he'd found for me. He pops round all the time to check I'm ok, he's one of the loveliest people I've ever met.

JOHN

I think you're right; who else do you like

TRACY

Well David's very nice but I think he's gay so I don't fancy him.

JOHN

He's not gay, he's just lonely, anyone else.

TRACY

Oliver, the black boy in the chorus, I could fancy him. He's got the most fabulous body, the trouble is he knows it and I have a feeling he might not be the most loyal boyfriend to have.

JOHN

You know who I fancy in this company.

TRACY

No.

JOHN

You.

TRACY

You're winding me up; you don't really, do you.

JOHN

I've been nuts about you since the first day I saw you in rehearsals.

TRACY

Why didn't you say something.

JOHN

Because I'm not like they portray me in the press; I am actually a very shy person.

TRACY

John; kiss me.

THEY KISS.

JOHN

Thanks.

TRACY

Where are we going from here.

JOHN

I don't know, but I do know wherever it is I want to be there with you.

TRACY

You need to know some things about me before you say that, I'm not what I seem, I've been an awful person, you need to know.

JOHN

Know what.

TRACY

You're obviously a very shy bloke and I don't want to hurt you;

I've had more men than you've had hot dinners. I used to have anorexia; you know what it's like in this business especially if you're a dancer. Then I went the other way and put on loads of weight and I lost my self respect, I couldn't see any man wanting to be with me; I became a complete slag. I threw myself at any man who came along just so I felt wanted. It took me years to become normal; I'm sorry but you should know.

JOHN

I don't care about your past there were reasons for the way you behaved, all I care about is our future. I think both of us have learned something very important about each other tonight. I shouldn't have believed the rumours about you and Trevor but you know what it's like if no one stops a rumour it tends to become truth.

I'm sorry I got it wrong about you and Trevor, I thought…

TRACY

Well you thought wrong.

JOHN

I'm sorry, I didn't mean to upset you.

TRACY

Well you did and you're going to have to pay for it.

JOHN

Ok, sorry, what do you want, flowers, dinner, what.

TRACY

Nothing so easy, when we finish the run you and I are going to get together and we're going to do a Chekhov or some risky fringe play and your agent is going to give it maximum publicity.

JOHN

Ok we will.

TRACY

Good.

JOHN

Tracy.

TRACY
What.

JOHN
I love you.

SCENE THREE THE THIRD NIGHT.

KNOCK ON THE DOOR

GWEN

Rosie, is it safe to come in.

ROSIE

Yes it's safe, of course it's safe.

GWEN

What do you mean, of course it's safe; the number of times I've come in here and found you in the middle of some sexual act with one of the band or some other poor soul you've dragged off the street.

ROSIE

Gwen dear, perhaps we need a do not disturb sign for the door.

GWEN

Do you mind, this is my dressing room as well as yours.

ROSIE

It's not my fault, I can't use my digs they keep complaining about the noise.

GWEN

I'm not surprised the way you scream; I'm surprised they haven't called the police thinking someone's being murdered.

ROSIE

It's not my fault I have multiple orgasms.

GWEN

That's because you're doing it with multiple partners. Lord alone knows what you were doing the last time I caught you with the two young boys from box office; frankly I'm amazed someone of your age is so flexible.

ROSIE

I do a lot of yoga.

GWEN

You do a lot of something.

ROSIE

You're only jealous.

GWEN

Not of your reputation; you know the band call you Rosie the bike because they've all ridden you.

ROSIE

If they want to get bitchy I'll tell you some things about the boys in the band. You know John the drummer, you wouldn't believe what a bad sense of rhythm he has. The only way to have sex with him is to lie him down and climb on top, then tell him I'll do the rhythm, you just lie back and think of England. Then there's massive Mike on the bass; he can only do it if you abuse him. He gets off when I take of my Dandini costume and walk all over him just dressed in the stockings suspenders and stiletto heels. Ask to see his bruises, he's not shy.

GWEN

I couldn't possibly.

ROSIE

I think you've led a sheltered life.

GWEN

I think, compared to you everyone's led a sheltered life.

ROSIE

I've had a twosome with Stan on trombone and Jack on trumpet; you can't believe what they can do with their lips, it must be something to do with all that puckering they do.

GWEN

I'm never sure if you don't just make this stuff up.

ROSIE

Oh no, you can't make this up; the only one I've not had in the band is Simon. You know he's in the BNP, well he uses prostitutes, black ones; it's the only way he can get it on, he absolutely hates it and he's terrified that people will find out. There must be some deep seated phycological reason but I'm dammed if I know what it is. Perhaps he had a miss spent youth reading all those old National Geographic magazines with the naked tribeswomen. I know I stole them from the school library when I was a girl; very stimulating.

GWEN

You're beyond help, you are.

ROSIE

No I'm not, all I need is some more help from Oliver the gorgeous young black boy in the chorus, he's divine. He's also hung like a donkey and so obliging, if I wasn't old enough to be his mother I'd seriously consider becoming monogamous.

GWEN

Rosie, you're just so tacky, sometimes I find you embarrassing beyond belief.

ROSIE

Don't have a go at me; people who live in glass houses shouldn't throw stones.

GWEN

And why do I live in a glass house.

ROSIE

Gwen dear, are you joking; I'm sorry but just look at the way your children treat you, what you put up with there leaves me lost for words. No wonder you always get cast as the Fairy Godmother. There's not a week goes by without your Justin coming in here demanding money with menaces. If he acted like that with anyone else they'd have him arrested.

GWEN

He's always asked for money like that, I'm used to it; it looks worse than it is.

ROSIE

Worse than it is; he stands up in your face and pushes you around the room, I've seen how terrified you are of him.

GWEN

It was my fault I left their father when they were just teenagers they must have felt awful. I destroyed their lives, I'm the guilty one, it's my fault.

ROSIE

What the Hell are you talking about, you're guilty; you left a man who was physically and mentally abusing you and you think you're the guilty one. Get real here, where do you think your children have got it from; like father like son.

GWEN

I know you're right, but I can't stop feeling I'm guilty, it's just the way I am.

ROSIE

No, it's the way you've been conditioned to feel; if you've been constantly beaten down and told you're useless for years it's hardly surprising you believe it after all this time.

GWEN

I don't know how to change.

ROSIE

Well we're going to have to find a way; it's hard to believe you're such a successful actor, you've been in everything, now you're the star of Grange Road and yet you let your children walk all over you.

GWEN

I know, it's pitiful isn't it.

ROSIE

Yes it is, but I've got the solution; you're a brilliant actor, I think we need to do some improv; some role play where you take control. Come on lets give it a go.

GWEN

Ok, I'll try.

ROSIE

Right I'll play your son; ready.

GWEN

Ok; action.

ROSIE

Hi ma, give me some money, ma give me some money, come on I need some money. I need it now, give me the money don't mess me around.

GWEN

Would you please let go of my arms, you're hurting me.

ROSIE

I'm not going to let go until you give me some money, come on give me some money; I'll go away as soon as you give me the money. Give me the money; now.

GWEN

Please stop you're hurting me.

ROSIE

Gwen, stop this, you're supposed to be acting and you're just being yourself; you're just being a victim.

GWEN

I'm sorry but you scared me it was just like when Justin scares me.

ROSIE

You know what the problem is Justin is a bully, just like his father and the thing to know about most bullies is that underneath they're cowards. Now lets try again.

GWEN

I'm sorry, you're right.

ROSIE

Ok, so; give me the money, Ma give me the money, I'll go away as soon as you give me the money. Come on I want money; now.

GWEN

SHOUTING

Let go of me, let go of me Justin, I mean it, I mean it now. I've had enough of your bullying. Leave me alone, Justin.

ROSIE

That's better, see, you can do it.

GWEN

Yes I can, you're right I can; it's time to put a stop to this, pass me the phone.

DIALING

Hello, Jason, it's your mother here; now don't say anything I have something important I want to say and you need to listen. I said listen. I've had enough Jason, I've had enough of your bullying ways and I'm not putting up with it anymore. You've picked up your violent temper from your father and I should have stopped you years ago; well better late than never. Jason, shut up. Listen to me Jason; don't you ever come demanding money from me ever again. If you do I swear I will call the police and have you arrested. If you or your brothers want to see me I will see you on my terms, that is properly and respectfully. Do you understand. Good. Goodbye Jason.

ROSIE

My God Gwen, I knew you were a good actor but that was brilliant.

GWEN

No it wasn't; I wasn't acting.

ROSIE

I don't know about you but I could do with a drink.

GWEN

Yes I think that would be a good idea, open the wine; look my hands are shaking.

ROSIE

I'm not surprised I'm a bit in shock myself.

GWEN

You know I've been so foolish I should have done that years

ago, you were right I was bullied, I was bullied all my married life. When I look back I can see where I went wrong; my husband was such a waste of space. I carried him all through our married life and yet he made me feel like I was the useless one. It wasn't me that had affairs, it wasn't me down the pub all the time. He just treated me like a skivvy to look after him and the kids. I've been taken for a ride all along; well now, thanks to you that's all over.

ROSIE

I've never told anyone this before, but I was married once.

GWEN

You married, I don't believe it.

ROSIE

I can hardly believe it myself, it was such a long time ago. He was from the same mould that your husband came from except he was worse. It all starts in such a subtle way, they get control of you before you've realised what they're doing. Little things like criticising your cooking, undermining your confidence in everything you do to the point where you believe it's all your fault. I used to cook him meals every night, if I had a pound for every one he threw at the wall I'd be rich.

The mad thing is, he comes home drunk throws your food at the wall and you're the one who feels guilty and apologises and cleans up the mess. Some nights if I was lucky he'd fall asleep in the chair before he threw the food, other nights I'd have the option of a good slapping or having sex. Actually the option was a good slapping or being raped, or some nights both. The tragic thing is you eventually accept all this as normal and even worse you accept it as your fault, I wouldn't have treated an animal the way my husband treated me. He'd frequently humiliate me in front of my friends, to the point that in the end I didn't have any friends; he was my only friend. How bizarre is that, my abuser became my only friend. I suffered his abuse for years, the police didn't get involved in domestics in those days, though God knows they came often enough. It would always be a male copper and my husband would say, oh she's been getting out of order and deserved a slap. As long as things were pacified they would leave and I would quietly submit to yet another rape from the man I had grown to hate. The trouble is you hate and fear them in equal measure, so how can you get away. I had a girlfriend in the same situation, she tried to leave and he found her and threw acid in her face. He's in prison now, but she's disfigured for life and petrified in case he finds her when he comes out and we're supposed to live in a civilised society. I've become involved with the battered wives refuge; if you spent a day listening to some of their stories it would break your heart. There have been far too many honour killings just lately and they're just the tip of the iceberg. For every death there are at least ten suicides, young girls who are in love with someone the family won't accept, scared to death they will be sent home to marry someone they haven't even met. What a sad waste of a young life and the worse thing is lots of men get away with it such is the climate of fear they create, people are too frightened to testify against them.

I've known that fear, I've been hospitalised by my ex too many times to remember, that's why I hated to see the way Jason was treating you. The last time my husband hit me I ended up in intensive care and yet I still went back. I told him I'd give him one last chance and what does he do two months later; well this time I'd had enough. We were in the kitchen and I grabbed a knife and I stabbed him.

GWEN

My God, Rosie, what happened.

ROSIE

I hit an artery; I didn't mean to I was just lashing out to protect myself, he was a brute, he deserved it.

GWEN

What happened.

ROSIE

He died; I watched him bleed to death in front of me, I watched him screaming and squirming on the kitchen floor. You know what I felt.

GWEN

What.

ROSIE

Nothing, I felt nothing.

GWEN

What happened to you.

ROSIE

I got ten years.

GWEN

My God Rosie how did you cope with that.

ROSIE

The same way you cope with the beatings; you can get used to anything if you have to. The only good thing about prison, was the sex, as long as you're broad minded; I'd never thought of myself as lesbian but inside it's different. I was locked up from the beginning, I didn't get bail; you can't imagine the shock when you go inside for the first time. The first night I shared a cell with a prostitute who was addicted to crack, she scared the life out of me but I suppose she must have been scared to death of me too, after all I was in for murder.

Gradually you get used to it and by the time you're sentenced you've become institutionalised. The thing that got me through it was the friendship and support of the other girls, some in a mental way and some physical. I had more sex in prison than I had before when I was being raped by my husband all the time. The difference was of course inside it was by choice; I still prefer sex with a man but my God some of those girls had some imagination when it came to sex. I only served six years what with time served and remission, I came out changed my name and got on with my life; in many ways it was worth it to be rid of him.

GWEN

I'm so sorry I had no idea, I shouldn't have been so critical of your lifestyle.

69

ROSIE

That's ok, we all have our ways of coping with life.

GWEN

Maybe there's more to your way than I thought.

ROSIE

It does put a smile on your face every now and then; you ought to try it. I'll tell you what I'll set you up on a date with Colepepper you could do with some love in your life. Ok.

GWEN

Yes, yes ok Rosie, thanks.

SCENE FOUR. THE FOURTH NIGHT.

KNOCK AT THE DOOR

DONALD
> Hello Wayne old boy, are you there.

WAYNE
> Yes I'm here where else would I be.

DONALD
> I've no idea, but it's just polite to ask.

WAYNE
> How are you tonight Donald.

DONALD
> Well actually I'm in a delightful mood, although I'm a little tired.

WAYNE
> And what have you been up to that should make you so tired.

DONALD
> Well old chap, for the first time in years I had a date.

WAYNE
> A date eh, who with.

DONALD
> With Gwen.

WAYNE
> Gwen, who.

DONALD
> Gwen Thomas; Fairy Godmother Gwen.

WAYNE
> Really, and did you have a good time.

DONALD
> Absolutely fabulous, I haven't had such a good time in years. I'd

71

forgotten what it was like to go out with a woman on a one to one basis. She's such a nice person she seems to have blossomed all of a sudden. We went to the Italian in George Lane; we chatted all night. It made me feel like a young man again and the best thing is we're going to do it again; I can't wait I'm like an excited schoolboy.

WAYNE

Did you get your leg over then Donald.

DONALD

I can't believe you would ask such a question. No I didn't, although I do believe if I'd had the chance I could have done.

WAYNE

You old devil, so tell me more.

DONALD

There's not much more to tell; we chatted all night, I haven't felt so relaxed with someone for years. She told me all sorts about her life and may I say I reciprocated. I haven't been that open with anyone for years. I found it a very cathartic experience, she helped me to let go, to open up. Thirty five years ago my wife was killed in a car accident and last night with Gwen was the first time I've spoken to anyone about it since it happened.

WAYNE

I'm so sorry Donald, I didn't know.

DONALD

That's awfully sweet of you old boy but you don't have to worry, after last night I can talk about it with anyone. I'd always been a shy old bugger so I was getting on a bit when we married but it was the best day of my life; I've never loved anyone like I loved Dorothy. Then to put the icing on the cake not long after we found out she was pregnant, I couldn't have been happier. Shortly after that I got Henry five with the RSC at Stratford upon Avon, how much better could life get. Dorothy drove me up and stayed to do some sightseeing while I was in rehearsals, it was one of the best times of my life. She went back on opening night; I told her to wait and go back in the morning but she had an early meeting the next day so she went back that evening after the party. I was woken in the early hours by a policeman who told me Dorothy had been involved in an accident and had died at the scene. My life fell apart; in that moment my wife and baby were dead and I didn't have the where with all to deal with it. The only way I could deal with it was to immerse myself in work; wasn't it Oscar Wilde who said; I love acting, it's so much more real than life.

I know I keep quoting Gielgud and Olivier and a lot of this company think I'm a sad old fart but that was a very important part of my life. Working with Johnny, Laurence and Ralphy at the RSC was the high light of my career and yet the lowest point of my life. I could have killed myself at the drop of a hat and yet the applause and the adrenalin kept me going. I kept all that sadness bottled up for years and then last night in Gwen's digs I let go of it all.

WAYNE
Oh, in Gwen's digs was it.

DONALD
Yes it was and I know how your brain works, so yes we did spend the night together, what was left of it. We had a cuddle in bed, naked, it was heaven.

WAYNE
No wonder you're in such a good mood, I'm really pleased for you, I hope it works out ok for you both.

DONALD
Thank you Wayne, I hope things work out for you to.

WAYNE
Work out for me.

DONALD
I do know Wayne and if there's anything I can do to help.

WAYNE
Know, what.

DONALD

I know about your dementia; it was obvious to me I've seen the signs before with my uncle. I know you're desperately trying to hide it, that's why I always try to help you with your lines.

WAYNE

I didn't think it showed.

DONALD

It doesn't yet to the others, they just think you're an arrogant old pop star milking it for all it's worth. I'm sure I'm the only one who realises you're just doing it because you can't remember the lines. When were you diagnosed.

WAYNE

Last year; they prescribed Donepezil which initially seemed to slow it down but lately it seems to be getting worse again.

DONALD

And the prognosis.

WAYNE

I don't know; well they don't know, except of course it's going to get worse.

DONALD

I'm very sorry old chap.

WAYNE

That's ok Donald, in some ways it's a relief to tell someone about it.

DONALD

Yes, a problem shared is a problem halved.

WAYNE

I'm afraid Donald, I'm really scared for the future, my mother had it, I know what it can do to you. I feel so sorry for my sister she had to look after her, I was lucky to be working away all the time. My mother deteriorated from a fit healthy old person to a shell in six years, my sister went through hell in that time. Mother started to loose her physical abilities first, it started with being unable to walk the dog or get to the shops. It seemed to have come on so suddenly; it was after she had a fall in the street, they took her to hospital but could find nothing wrong except her blood pressure was a little high. They sent her home but it was the start of her slow deterioration. Gradually she became more and more dependent on my sister to the point where my sister was her full time carer. Every day mother would loose her wedding ring and they would spend hours searching for it before she could pacify her. Eventually my sister took it from her for safe keeping so then she started to loose the keys for the house, there was always something mad going on. Mother started to see things, she'd see a young girl behind the couch or people climbing the walls, she'd be terrified.

Some days sis could calm her down by telling her it wasn't real, it was her brain playing tricks with her and she'd be ok, but other days there would be nothing she could do to pacify her. I don't know how my sister coped being on call twenty four hours a day; she'd get calls from the police to say they had found mother walking the streets in her nightie, it was frightening anything could have happened to her. Eventually my sister had to move in to be there full time, by now mother had lost control of her bladder, she'd be standing there talking and just piss herself. My sister persevered for years because she'd promised mother she wouldn't put her in a home. It would have driven me mad, in fact I think my sister was close to a nervous breakdown. She phoned me one night to say she'd locked herself out of the house and couldn't work out how to get back in, she was crying uncontrollably. All she had to do was go to the next door neighbours who had a spare key, but she couldn't work it out for herself. Thank God not long after that mother had another fall and was taken into hospital, they thought she'd had a stroke. It was the final straw she had to go into a nursing home, she was virtually a vegetable. My sister visits her every day except Sunday, she gives herself one day a week off. I don't know why she goes, it's got to the point that mother has no idea she's there; she hasn't opened her eyes for almost six months and when she speaks it's completely incomprehensible. I think my sister is so conditioned to going every day she doesn't know how to stop. She's still in the nursing home unable to do anything for herself, shitting in a nappy like a baby. I don't want to end up like that.

DONALD

It hasn't come to that yet, that's a long way off old chap, in the mean time there's not much I can do to help, the only thing I can suggest is to be honest with everyone else, at least then everyone can help you with your lines.

WAYNE

Yeah, thanks for the line prompts, it does help. You know I'm so pleased you've got together with Gwen, I knew her years ago. She was in my film Summer Weekend and she was a very nice girl and I mean that literally. She was virtually the only girl I didn't sleep with on that job, after all I was the star, they were lining up outside my dressing room. Gwen was better than the others she had the integrity to say no.

DONALD

Well that's nice to know.

WAYNE

You know who else was on that film, Norman Allen; that was in his hay day when he and Bert Baxter used to have their TV show The Comedy Hour. It's amazing now to think that celebrities were queuing to appear on their show to be humiliated by those two fools. They had Shirley Bassey on and they did a black and white minstrel act.

DONALD

Yes, indeed, I know they had Johnny Gielgud on and as you may know he was convicted for persistently importuning for immoral purposes, or picking up a man in a public toilet, cottaging as they call it nowadays. So predictably all the jokes were taking the mickey out of gay people; the trouble was you had to go on even if you didn't want to. Can you imagine the press in those days, if they'd found out you were asked and had refused.

WAYNE

The sad thing is they're still using the same gags today.

DONALD

I must say I'm not a fan of them at all, their material is so sexist.

WAYNE

Yes especially Normans, but there's a reason why he's so sexist, it's a front.

DONALD

How do you mean.

WAYNE

He's gay.

DONALD

I know there were rumours in the business, but what about his wife.

WAYNE

She was his secretary, he just married her as a front, he'd been living with his manager for years. They all used to live together in that big house in Totteridge next door to Adam Faith. I was friends with Adam in those days so I used to get all the gossip. They both used the same gardening company which was mostly staffed by fit young men. Normans wife Ellen had sex with nearly all of them at one time or another, sometimes two at once, apparently she was insatiable, it's no wonder the garden looked so unkempt. They did say that while all this was going on Norman and his manager Brian were frequently seen arguing around the swimming pool; Brian dressed in a blonde wig, pink dress and white sling backs, just like Doris Day, except for the moustache.

DONALD

Blimey

WAYNE

It was only a couple of years ago when his manager died that he divorced his secretary, he still won't come out though. Perhaps we all have our skeletons in the cupboard.

DONALD

I suppose you know mine, now what's yours.

WAYNE

Mine Donald, I don't have one.

DONALD

I'm sure with your miss spent youth there must be something.

WAYNE

What's this, true confessions, get it off my chest before it's too late, before I've lost my mind.

DONALD

Well perhaps, if you have something to confess, now would be a good time.

WAYNE

Ok Donald, you and I are more alike than you would imagine, remember I said I'd had every girl on Summer Weekend, well there was one in particular who I fell in love with, her name was Wendy. I would have married her if I'd had the chance, but in those days it was the kiss of death to a young pop stars career, we had to be seen to be available. Looking back it's ridiculous but that's how it was then; anyway one day Wendy came to me and said she was pregnant, I was just a kid, just starting my career, I couldn't have anything jeopardize that. I gave her the money to get rid of it but she couldn't bring herself to do it. I told her that if she had

the child never to name me as the father as I would deny it and she would look like a fool. She must have felt so rejected she threw herself in front of an underground train and killed herself. I was the one who was the fool, I should have had the guts to stand by her. Like you Donald, the love of my life was dead; no one connected her with me, there were just a few lines in the paper; young dancer killed in tragic accident. I did exactly the same as you, I worked myself to death. That's why everyone thought I was so arrogant, because all I thought about was me and my career.

DONALD

It wasn't your fault Wayne, that was the way things were in those days, we're all victims of our circumstances.

WAYNE

I know you're right but it's hard to move on, even now.

DONALD

Hard, but not impossible; you're right we are surprisingly alike and yet so different. We've both lost someone we love, someone who meant everything to us and have both taken far too long to come out the other side. I've come through it with Gwens help, now it's your turn to let go of the past. It wasn't your fault, we were both victims, but like me it's now time for you to stop being a victim and move on.

WAYNE

You're right Donald, it is time for me to move on.

DONALD

I'll tell you what, I'm going for a meal after the show with Gwen, come with us old chap. Nothing heavy, nothing pressured, just a drink and a meal with friends who care.

WAYNE

Thanks Donald, I'd love to.

SCENE FIVE. THE LAST NIGHT.

KNOCK AT THE DOOR

NORMAN
Come in.

BERT
How do I get in.

NORMAN
Turn the knob on your side.

BERT
I haven't got a knob on my side.

THE DOOR OPENS

NORMAN
Goon Show 1960, I'll name that gag in one.

BERT
Evening Norman, dead right, although I think you'll find the year was 1959.

NORMAN
Yes Bert, I bow to your superior knowledge you're right Eccles and Bluebottle 1959.

BERT
I can't believe this was the last night, it seems to have flown by.

NORMAN
Well it was a fairly good company this year, that helps.

BERT
Have you been with the same company as me, some of them are the most boring people I've ever had the misfortune to meet.

NORMAN
Who.

BERT

Colepepper, God if I have to listen to another of his; when I was at the RSC with Johnny and Ralphy speeches.

NORMAN

He's a sad old bugger but he means well.

BERT

What about the two fools in the panto horse, I'm sure they're an affair, they're always skulking around together.

NORMAN

I sometimes wonder about you; you can be such a bitchy old queen yourself.

BERT

Bitchy moi, how about Gwen, no wonder she's always on her own. God knows I like a fag, but she's like a bloody chimney.

NORMAN

What about Rosie, I thought you two might get together, there was a rumour she was a nymphomaniac.

BERT

I'm sure she is, that's why I hate her; she rejected me, I've no idea why.

NORMAN

She's very deep, that one.

BERT

Unlike Tracy Phillips, she's such an air head, what's wrong with young people today, all they think about is their looks.

NORMAN

Perhaps it's a lesson we could learn from.

BERT

Not at my age, we can't, I'm old I'm balding and I've a beer gut; it took years of abuse to get to look like this. There is no way I want to go back to the way I was when I was young. When you're young you can do all night what it takes you all night to do when you're old, that's the only good thing about being young. Old man of eighty decides to take a Thai bride, all his friends are worried about his health.

NORMAN

So he goes to the doctors for a check up and the doctor warns him about the dangers of violent sexual activity and the possibility of a heart attack.

BERT

So the old man says; well if she dies she dies.

NORMAN

I thought you got on with John he's a young thrusting Prince Charming, just like you were when you were his age.

BERT

Are you sure, I never did drugs, well only fags and booze, I may have been thrusting but I've never been charming in my life.

NORMAN

Wayne's ok, I worked with him on Summer Weekend, he was fun.

BERT

He might have been fun then, but now he's a pain in the arse. Milking every scene for all he's worth, why he can't stick to the script God knows, anyone would think he's got dementia.

NORMAN

Well we've had a laugh, haven't we.

BERT

Yeah, I suppose so. Mans idea of safe sex.

NORMAN

Padded head board. I married Miss Right.

BERT

I hadn't realised her first name was always.

NORMAN

I haven't spoken to the wife for eighteen months.

TOGETHER

I didn't like to interrupt her.

NORMAN

I can still enjoy sex at 74.

BERT

I live at 75 so it's no distance. I want to die in my sleep like my father.

NORMAN

Not screaming and terrified like the passengers on his bus.

BERT

They're proper gags, not like this modern rubbish. It's come to something when there's more things you can't make gags about than things you can. The only people who can crack Jewish gags have to be Jewish, don't get me going about black gags, that was half my act. I hate to think what would happen if you cracked a gag about the wife or the mother in law, I can't stand all this political correctness.

NORMAN

You know what we are, dinosaurs; all our feeding grounds have gone and we're slowly dying out. All the pubs and working mens clubs are closing, you're looked on as a leper if you have a fag in the street; God forbid anyone should dare to light up in the pub. It's all well and good for those politicians to ban smoking but it was our living. What the hell was wrong with a smoke filled club, we all chose to go there, Les Dawson had it right, you can't die of nothing.

BERT

He used to do some fabulous gags, remember Cissie and Ada, him and Roy Barraclough dressed as women. That was a class act, I wanted to steal his Over The Garden wall act for us when he died but it seemed disrespectful. Take her at number fourteen, she's no better than she should be. Too thick with her lodger for my liking.

NORMAN

Well I heard her bed springs going at three o'clock this morning and her husbands on regular nights.

BERT

Yes, he was magic; I went to the doctors to get something for persistent wind, he gave me a kite.

NORMAN

I took my mother in law to Madame Tussards Chamber of Horrors and the attendant said keep her moving sir, we're stock taking.

BERT

You know he left his dressing room in The Empire Theatre in Sunderland vowing never to work there again. He never said why, although it's supposed to be haunted by the ghost of Sid James who died of a heart attack in the building.

BERT

Ironic that Les died of a heart attack not long after. Want a fag Norm.

NORMAN

Yeah, I'm gagging.

BERT

Here you are.

NORMAN

Thanks Bert; this is ridiculous, here we are two grown men, senior citizens, skulking around by an open window to have a fag like two naughty school boys.

BERT

How are the mighty fallen.

NORMAN

You've got a point, when we were doing The Comedy Hour we used to smoke on the set.

BERT

Yeah, happy days, we were the best, there was no one to touch us. What's blue and fluffy.

NORMAN

Blue fluff. There was a knock at the door, I knew it was the mother in law because the mice were throwing themselves on the traps.

BERT

The wife said, how would you like to talk to mummy, I said through a spiritualist.

NORMAN

Mixed feelings is when you see your mother in law driving over a cliff in your new car.

BERT

My mother in law has come to our house at Christmas seven years running. This year we're having a change.

NORMAN

We're going to let her in.

BERT

Yeah, the good old days, we had chauffeur driven limos then, what have we got now.

NORMAN

Our bus passes and our memories; we've known each other for so long we're like an old married couple, we even…

BERT

Finish each others sentences. I said to my neighbour; take my wife, now they've gone away together.

NORMAN

I don't half miss him.

BERT

Well you should know.

NORMAN
    Know what.

BERT
    Norman, it's five years since Brian died.

NORMAN
    Brian my manager.

BERT
    No Norman, Brian your lover.

NORMAN
    I can't believe you said that, I thought you were my friend.

BERT
    I am your friend, that's why I said it. Don't you think it's time to come clean.

NORMAN
    Don't you mean come out; how can I come out it will ruin my career.

BERT
    Your career. Norm your career and mine went down the pan years ago when they invented political correctness. Out of the two of us you're the one with a chance of a career if you do come out. Look at Frankie Howerd he rose from the ashes more times than the Phoenix and you both went to the same rug maker.

NORMAN
    How dare you, do you know how much I paid for this syrup.

BERT
    Too much.

NORMAN
    Don't mock Francis.

BERT
    There you are, you can do it, that's your new career sorted.

NORMAN

I think I need a lot more rehearsals before I can pull that off.

BERT

That's ok, we can work on it, I'll be your manager, although I'll just stick to the manager bit, I'm not Brian. I'll leave the shirt lifting to you.

NORMAN

That's a bit politically incorrect Bert.

BERT

Like I care, I'm too bloody old to change now, you were right, we are dinosaurs.

NORMAN

It's a funny old business being a comedian.

BERT

No, it's actually deadly serious.

NORMAN

You're right, so many of them have committed suicide, look at poor old Hancock.

BERT

Yeah, Tony was a beautiful man, too fragile for this business. Drunk himself to death consumed with self doubt about his talent, so sad. They published his suicide letter; it said, things went wrong too many times.

NORMAN

My friend Kenny Williams, tortured soul he was. He was like me he never came out, even though everyone knew he was gay. I never did a Carry On, but they say Charles Hawtrey was worse; he was a drunken promiscuous old queen who smoked and drunk himself to death.

BERT

We're lucky at least we survived.

NORMAN

Do you have any regrets Bert.

BERT

Loads, and you.

NORMAN

One or two; you're right I should have come out ages ago.

BERT

I'm surprised you haven't been caught by the press.

NORMAN

There have been the odd; Friend of Dorothy stories, perhaps I'm not a big enough story any more.

BERT

Anything else.

NORMAN

Well, yes, remember all those years ago I was in Wayne Peters film Summer Weekend. He got one of the young dancers pregnant and told her to get rid of it. She came to me for advice and I told her to think of her career and get rid of it. She was such a delicate thing and I was so hard on her, she looked upon me as a father figure and I let her down. When I found out she'd committed suicide I was devastated, it was as if I'd lost a child myself. Then later when Brian died that's when I should have come out, not pretending he was just my manager. You have now idea how I hated his funeral, I wanted to shout out, he was the man I loved. The man who had devoted his life to me was dead and I didn't have the guts to say I loved him. That's my biggest regret.

BERT

We all have our regrets, I was a right bastard in the early days, I'd do anything to get a job. You know how homophobic the old bookers were especially in the northern clubs, well I'd start a rumour that some of the acts were gay, it's amazing how soon their bookings drop. I did it to Eric, you know Eric Shirvell, back of the horse. We were up for a commercial and I told the director Eric had aids. I know he never worked for that director again; I wonder if he ever found out what I'd done, I must ask him one day. He wasn't the only one I did that trick on, I was an absolute bastard.

NORMAN

Did you ever do that to me.

BERT

No, you were a bloody good comedian, better than me that's why I wanted to work with you. You know how we got together as a double act.

NORMAN

Yes, my agent suggested we'd work well as a double act and he'd already had a tentative offer for a TV show.

BERT

Actually, that's close but no cigar, it was me who set the whole thing up. I set up the TV deal, then told them to speak to your agent to sort it out. I always was a manipulating so and so, that's why I was always top dog in the act even though you were a better comic.

NORMAN

Well you learn something every day, you cunning bugger,

BERT

That's one of the best things I ever managed to arrange, I've never had a moments regret about our partnership it was the best thing I ever did.

NORMAN

Blimey Bert, I never knew you cared.

BERT

Well now you know.

NORMAN

Come on let's go or we'll be late for the party.

BERT

There's no rush, it will be the same old rubbish as last year. Trevor going on about what a wonderful company it's been this year and how he's really looking forward to working with us again next year and it will sound like he really means it.

NORMAN

Perhaps he does, I know I do. Come on we've a party to go to.

THE DOOR OPENS

AND THEY EXIT

NEIGHBOURHOOD WATCH.

A GROUP OF PEOPLE ARE SEEN IN THE DISTANCE
WALKING DOWN THE STREET.
DIANE IN A WHEELCHAIR IS BEING PUSHED BY
JACK. BRENDA WALKS BEHIND WITH TOM WHO IS
CARRYING A VERY LARGE BUNDLE IN A SACK
OVER HIS SHOULDER.

THE WHEELCHAIR BUMPS DOWN A FLIGHT OF
STAIRS AND STOPS AT THE DOOR AT THE
BOTTOM

DIANE

    Why didn't we find one without stairs.

BRENDA

    KISSING HER TEETH.

    Don't be daft Diane you can't have a cellar without stairs.

DIANE

    Of course not, silly me.

    THE DOOR OPENS AND THEY ALL ENTER AND
    TURNING ON THE FAIRLY DIM LIGHTING THEY
    CONGREGATE IN THE CENTRE OF THE ROOM.

    TOM PLACES THE SACK HE WAS CARRYING ON THE
    FLOOR.

JACK

    Anyone for tea.

DIANE

    Yes please I'm parched.

    JACK DISAPPEARS INTO ANOTHER ROOM.

DIANE

    Are you sure this is a good idea.

TOM

    Of course it is, we've already agreed it is, there's no going back
    now.

BRENDA
  Yes, we're all in this together.

DIANE
  Are you alright Jack, do you want a hand.

JACK
  No thanks, I'm fine, I won't be long.

THE DOOR OPENS AND JACK ENTERS PUSHING A TEA TROLLEY, HE STOPS AND STARTS TO ORGANISE THE TEA.

JACK
  Now who's for milk and sugar.

TOM PLACES TWO CHAIRS AND A TEA CHEST CLOSE TO THE TROLLEY. TOM SITS ON THE CHEST AND BRENDA TAKES ONE OF THE CHAIRS.

BRENDA
  I'm white, no sugar, I'm watching my weight, thanks.

TOM
  Me too.

DIANE
  I'll live dangerously, milk and sugar, please.

JACK
  Fig roll anyone.

TOM
  A what.

JACK
  Fig roll.

TOM
  Sounds awful, haven't you any normal biscuits.

JACK
  Yes, of course, I've loads of stuff, I'm just rather partial to fig

rolls myself. Here look, Rich Tea, Bourbon, Chocolate Fingers. I thought we might be here for quite a while so I stocked up there's tons of food in the kitchen.

TOM

Well done Jack, it's important to have a good supply officer.

BRENDA

It's important that we all work together as a team.

DIANE

Yes we all have our parts to play. All the worlds a stage.

TOM

What.

DIANE

Oh, it's Shakespeare.

TOM

Oh yeah I remember him, not that I remember much. What was that story of the battle where we thrashed the French. Once more unto the breach dear friends.

DIANE

Well Tom, you obviously remember more than you thought.

TOM

It's funny the things you remember, I often thought of Once more unto the breach when I was in Afghanistan. That's the proper way to fight, not like those Taliban bastards. I've seen too many of my mates killed and maimed by IED's. That's not proper fighting, blokes getting their arms and legs blown off and ending up a bloody cripple in a wheel chair. Oh, I'm sorry I didn't mean...

DIANE

It's ok Tom, I know what you mean.

THERE IS A LOW GROANING NOISE FROM THE SACK ON THE FLOOR.

JACK

Looks like laughing boy is waking up.

WAYNE

FROM THE SACK

What the fuck, what the fuck, oh my fucking head. Where am I.

TOM GOES OVER AND OPENS THE SACK.

TOM

Hello Wayne, you're in the shit, that's where you are.

WAYNE

Who the fuck are you.

TOM GRABS WAINE HANDCUFFS HIM AND CHAINS HIM TO THE HEAVY RADIATOR.

TOM

I'm Tom, and I'm a fuck site bigger and stronger than you are, anything else you want to know.

WAYNE

You can't do this to me you cunt.

TOM

I think you'll find we can. We can do anything we want and you'd better get used to it Wayne.

WAYNE

You bastards, how did I get here.

JACK

LAUGHING AND SHOWING TRANQUILISER GUN.

You know what Wayne; you're such a light weight. We took you down with an animal tranquiliser gun.

WAYNE

You bastards.

JACK

Yeah, your so tough we knocked you out with a dose for a koala bear, a little fluffy koala bear. That's how tough you are Wayne.

WAYNE

You wouldn't say that to me if I wasn't chained up here. I'll fucking stab you, you bastard.

JACK

What makes you think I'm scared of you I've fought in the Falklands and you think I'm afraid of a little shit like you.

WAYNE

Yeah well you might not be scared but there's plenty of others who shit themselves when they see me. When I walk down the street and bump into people they say sorry.

JACK

You stupid little boy, this is Britain, everyone says sorry when they bump into people, even if it's not their fault.

TOM

I'll tell you what Wayne, just chill out, this is going to be a long wait for you and you really don't want to upset us in the mean time.

BRENDA

Ok, I'm cooking tonight. I'm doing chicken rice and peas, curried goat, plantin, ocra and Guinness punch.

DIANE

Sounds great.

BRENDA GOES TO THE KITCHEN.

WAYNE

I'm not eating that shit.

DIANE

You don't know what you're missing

WAYNE

I don't give a shit I want some proper English food I want burger and chips.

DIANE

I'm sure we can sort out a burger for you but it's your loss.

WAYNE

You lot are going to be in big trouble when my posse finds out where I am. They'll come here mob handed and tooled up.

JACK

I wouldn't hold your breath waiting on that Wayne, no one knows where you are.

JACK EXITS THE CELLAR

WAYNE

I'll phone them, then we'll see.

REACHING FOR HIS PHONE

You bastards, where's my phone.

TOM

Credit us with some intelligence Waine, we've planned this with military planning. You're fucked mate.

WAYNE

You can't do this to me, I've got my rights.

TOM

What like all the people you terrorised.

WAYNE

They asked for it, they were wankers.

TOM

You know what Wayne, I could have been like you, I could have wasted my life but I was saved. I was saved by the army. Why are you so angry Wayne.

WAYNE

I'm angry because of wankers like you who keep poking their fucking noses into my business

BRENDA COMES OUT OF THE KITCHEN CARRYING CUTLERY AND PLATES.

97

BRENDA
>Dinner won't be long.

TOM DRAGS TWO MORE TEA CHESTS OVER
PUSHING THEM TOGETHER TO MAKE A TABLE. HE
SETS THE TABLE WITH BRENDA WHO GOES BACK
TO THE KITCHEN WITH THE TROLLEY.

JACK ENTERS THE CELLAR WITH BURGER AND
CHIPS WHICH HE TAKES OVER TO WAYNE AND
PLACES IT ON THE FLOOR.

WAYNE
>Where's the fucking tomato sauce.

FRANK
>There's a sachet.

WAYNE
>I can't open that you fucking idiot.

FRANK
>You know you don't have to keep swearing.

FRANK GOES TO THE TABLE AND TAKES BACK A
BOTTLE OF KETCHUP AND PUTS IT ON WAYNES
CHIPS.

WAYNE
>Salt.

FRANK
>Don't push your luck Wayne, you're the one chained up not me.

FRANK GETS THE SALT FOR WAYNE.

BRENDA COMES IN WITH THE TROLLEY LADEN
WITH FOOD AND THEY ALL SIT DOWN AND EAT.

DIANE
>Thanks Brenda, this looks lovely.

TOM
>Yeah, this is fabulous, pass the chicken please Jack.

JACK

Here Tom, you must try the curry goat it just falls off the bone. You've done a great job here Brenda.

BRENDA

Thanks, I'm glad you're all enjoying it.

WAYNE

Looks like shit to me.

TOM

You know what Wayne, you don't know what you're missing.

WAYNE

I can't stand foreign shit.

TOM

Please yourself, but if I was on trial tomorrow I'd try to get some decent grub in me and a decent nights sleep. I have a feeling you're going to need all your energy for tomorrow.

WAYNE

What you talking about trial tomorrow.

TOM

Oh, didn't we mention your trial tomorrow.

WAYNE

On trial, on trial for fucking what.

TOM

For being a complete shit amongst other things.

JACK TAKES WAYNE SOME CANS OF LAGER.

JACK

Here Wayne, have some lager, just get quietly pissed and don't make a fuss. We don't want to have to use the tranquiliser gun again, do we.

BRENDA AND TOM CLEAR UP THE DINNER AND START SETTING UP SOME CAMP BEDS AND SLEEPING BAGS.

JACK CARRIES A CAMP BED AND SLEEPING BAG
OVER TO WAYNE.

WAYNE

What the fucks this.

JACK

It's your bed for the night. Now just give it a rest for a while and go to sleep like a good boy.

WAYNE

Don't fucking good boy me, this is wrong you can't do this. This is all wrong, I must be dreaming, I must have had some bad gear.

SHOUTING

Fuck off, fuck off, fuck off.

JACK

You know what Wayne I've had enough of you for one day.

HE PULLS THE TRANQUILISER GUN OUT AIMS AT WAYNE AND FIRES.

FADE TO BLACK

WAYNES POV WIDE SHOT PULL FOCUS ON EVERYONE SITTING EATING BREAKFAST.

JACK

Feeling better for your nights sleep young man.

WAYNE

Don't fucking young man me you stupid old fucker.

JACK

I may be old Wayne, but I'm not stupid and you may well find that out later today.

BRENDA

Come here and have some breakfast, here's a bacon roll, I assume you can manage that.

WAYNE SLOUCHES OVER AND SITS DOWN AND EATS

THE ROLL.

WAYNE STARTS TO TALK, BUT IN A MUCH MORE SUBMISSIVE WAY THAN BEFORE.

WAYNE

You lot are mad, I can't believe you had the bollocks to do this to me. When I'm out of here I'll find you and I'll make your life hell.

FRANK

And how are you going to do that eh Wayne, you have no idea where any of us live and you won't find us either. You and your posse never go further than a five mile radius, your life is tragic. You terrorise anyone in your area but when you step outside your patch you fall prey to rival gangs. I bet you've never been out of the country, I bet you don't even have a passport. Your world is so small and now it's about to come crashing down on you.

SUDDENLY THE FAR SIDE OF THE ROOM IS LIT UP REVEALING A MAKE SHIFT COURT ROOM MADE OF PACKING CASES AND OTHER RUBBISH. THE JURY IS MADE UP OF TWELVE MOP HEADS.

TOM DRAGS WAYNE TO THE DOCK AND HAND CUFFS HIS HANDS AND TIES HIS ANKLES.

TOM

Be upstanding for his honour Judge Jack Heath.

JACK ENTERS IN WIG AND GOWN AND SITS IN THE JUDGES SEAT.

JACK

And who appears for the defence.

BRENDA

IN WIG AND GOWN

I do, your honour.

JACK

And who appears for the prosecution.

DIANE

IN WIG AND GOWN

I do, your honour.

JACK

Ladies and gentlemen, this court is taking place today under our new neighbourhood watch, re claim the streets initiative.

TOM PLACES WAYNES HAND ON THE BIBLE AND HOLDS UP A CARD.

TOM

Please read the words on the card.

WAYNE

I can't read you arse hole.

TOM

Then I'll have to read it for you. I swear by almighty God that the evidence I shall give shall be the truth, the whole truth and nothing but the truth. Thank you Wayne.

DIANE

When did you first come to the attention of the police Wayne.

WAYNE

How should I know, they were always on my case as long as I can remember

DIANE

You are the son of Verna Bailey.

WAYNE

Yeah, Verna is my mum.

DIANE

And your father.

WAYNE

How should I know, he fucked off before I was born.

DIANE

It's not easy being the son of a single parent is it Wayne.

102

WAYNE

I aint got a clue, where I come from it's normal.

DIANE

So by your own admission being the son of a single parent is normal and therefore no defence for your crimes.

WAYNE

I've not been found guilty of any crimes except anti social behaviour, check my ASBO.

DIANE

I'm sure you're right Wayne, but just because you haven't been convicted doesn't mean you're not guilty. It is the prosecutions case that Wayne Bailey is guilty of numerous offences which have terrorised his neighbourhood and in one case has led to the death of a mother and her daughter.

I would like to start with the security camera footage from 12 Fortune Road, the house of Mr and Mrs Norman.

A FILM SCREEN DROPS DOWN AND THE FILM STARTS TO RUN, DURING WHICH TIME DIANE CONTINUES WITH HER EVIDENCE.

DIANE

As you can see here is footage of Wayne and his posse playing football outside the house of Mr and Mrs Norman and here Mrs Norman comes out to ask them to stop.

WAYNE

She was fucking mad, she told us we were Martians and told us to go back to our space ship.

DIANE

Did you go Wayne.

WAYNE

What, have some mad old cow tell us what to do, are you stupid or something. We left when we were ready.

DIANE

And you came back later, didn't you Wayne.

WAYNE

Might have done.

THE FILM RUNS AGAIN, THIS TIME IT'S NIGHT AND WAYNE AND HIS POSSE ARE OUTSIDE WITH TORCHES HIGHLIGHTING THEIR FACES AND DEELY BOPPERS ON THEIR HEADS. YOU HEAR THEM CHANT

WAYNES POSSE

Come on out you mad old cow, we're the Martians and we've come to get you.

DIANE

That's you in the film isn't it Wayne.

WAYNE

Might be, what's wrong with that she was a mad old cow she started it.

DIANE

That's a matter of opinion Wayne. Regardless of who started it, as you say, you kept on going back and tormenting Mrs Norman.

WAYNE

Mad old cow.

DIANE

I suppose she was in a way Wayne. Mrs Norman had dementia, do you know what that is.

WAYNE

I ain't got a fucking clue.

DIANE

It's a disease that old people get when their brain stops working properly. They become confused, they frequently become very scared because they can't understand what's going on. Mrs Norman really thought you and your friends were Martians from outer space and yet you persisted in going back time and time again to torment this frail old woman. She had to be taken into an old people's home in the end and would hide under the bed in case the Martians came for her. Three months later Mr Norman died of a heart attack, of course, none of this had anything to do with you, did it Wayne.

WAYNE

It weren't my fault, she was a mad old bastard.

THE FILM STARTS TO RUN AGAIN.

DIANE

Here's some more footage of you outside the newsagents shop owned by Mr Sagoo. We can see you and your friends clearly throwing eggs at him and his shop

WAYNE

So what, it's just eggs, it's just a laugh.

DIANE

I suppose you've no idea who went back later that night and poured petrol through the letter box. You do realise you could have killed Mr Sagoo and his family.

WAYNE

I never done it and anyway, why should I care he was just a stupid Paki.

DIANE

According to you Wayne, you seem to have led a completely blameless life, I'm amazed you managed to get an ASBO.

THE FILM STARTS TO RUN AGAIN, THIS TIME AN EXTREME CLOSE UP OF WAYNE SHOUTING.

WAYNE

Cripple, cripple, useless cripple.

DIANE

You can't deny that was you this time, can you Wayne.

WAYNE

Yeah it was me, like I give a shit.

DIANE

You were shouting at Vicky Edge and her mother Maureen who was her full time carer. Did you realise Vicky had cerebral palsy which was why she was in a wheelchair. They were scared to death of you.

THE FILM RUNS AGAIN SHOWING WAYNE SITTING ON THE WALL OUTSIDE THE EDGE HOUSE SMOKING A CIGARETTE.

WAYNE

What's wrong with that I'm just having a fag.

DIANE

You have no idea how you effected these people, have you Wayne.

WAYNE

I'm just having a fag.

DIANE

Well Wayne, you terrified Mrs Edge and her daughter so much that they left the area. They were so desperate to get away that they ended up living in Mrs Edge's car. Have you any idea how desperate someone must have been to live in a car with a child suffering from cerebral palsy.

WAYNE

I don't know, she was just some kid in a wheelchair.

DIANE

And you thought it was fair to terrorise them.

WAYNE

Yeah, if I hadn't of done it I would have looked weak and then some bastard would have had me.

DIANE

So, it's kill or be killed in your world Wayne.

WAYNE

Yeah, kill or be killed.

DIANE

Mrs Edge finally got to a point where she was at her wits end despairing of a way out. Sadly the only way out for her was to set fire to the car she and her daughter lived in. They both died of horrific burns. You may think that none of this was your fault Wayne, the prosecution would beg to differ. We rest our case your honour.

BRENDA

Now it falls upon me to present the case for the defence and I must say I'm not sure where to start.

THE FILM RUNS AGAIN SHOWING SHOTS OF WAYNE IN THE GARDEN AS A HAPPY YOUNG BOY.

BRENDA

You look so innocent there Wayne, it's hard to believe it's you.

WAYNE

It's not me, that's some kid who used to be me, I can't even remember him.

BRENDA

You look very happy there.

WAYNE

I told you, I can't even remember back then.

THE FILM RUNS AGAIN SHOWING A YOUNG BOY GOING TO SCHOOL.

BRENDA

How was school Wayne, were you still happy there.

WAYNE

I fucking hated school, I hated it from the very first day. At home I could do what I liked then all of a sudden I had some stupid bastard telling me to sit down, to pay attention, to stop talking. Even at that age I knew school was a waste of time, you don't need to read or write to earn money. My mums boyfriend used to get me to run errands for him, no copper stops a kid when they're looking for drugs. I earned shed loads. I hardly ever went to school they were a bunch of wankers, they excluded me in the end then we were all happy. So now I deal a bit, use a bit, I'm king of the castle. One day some cunt will take me out and he'll be top man but until then I'm the daddy. I don't expect to live past thirty and I don't want to, fuck it.

BRENDA

I don't think I could have put it better, you were indeed a victim of your circumstances.

WAYNE

Bollocks, I made the best of my circumstances.

BRENDA

Sadly, here ends the case for the defence.

JACK

Perhaps we should have a little break before I sum up the evidence, I think tea and biscuits would be a good idea.

TOM

Court rise.

THEY ALL STAND AND JACK WALKS TOWARDS THE KITCHEN AREA FOLLOWED BY EVERYONE EXCEPT WAYNE WHO IS STILL CHAINED TO THE CHAIR IN THE DOCK.

WAYNE

Oh, where you lot going.

TOM

We're having a tea break, what's it look like.

BRENDA AND TOM GO INTO THE KITCHEN.

WAYNE

And what about me.

DIANE

Don't worry Wayne we'll bring you one.

JACK SITS ON ONE OF THE PACKING CASES AND

DIANE WHEELS HER CHAIR NEXT TO HIM.

DIANE

I must say this is a lot harder than I expected. It seemed like it would be so simple, so straightforward. Now I'm not so sure.

JACK

Don't worry, I know what you mean, but we're doing the right thing. We're doing the right thing for Maureen and Vicky Edge, they're not here to fight for themselves. Perhaps if someone had been there for them they would have been here today.

DIANE

Yes of course, you're right, I was just loosing my nerve a bit.

JACK

It's ok, we're all in this together, we're doing the right thing.

TOM AND BRENDA COME OUT OF THE KITCHEN WITH THE TEA TROLLEY.

BRENDA

Tea's up.

THEY SIT DOWN AND POUR THE TEA INCLUDING ONE FOR WAYNE.

TOM CALLS TO WAYNE.

TOM

Sugar.

WAYNE

You talking to me.

TOM

Yes Wayne, sugar.

WAYNE

Yes please.

JACK

Blimey, that's the politest thing he's said since he's been here, perhaps we are getting through.

TOM WALKS OVER TO WAYNE WITH THE TEA.

TOM

There's some biscuits there too.

WAYNE

Thanks.

TOM

Well done Wayne, see you can be polite if you try hard enough.

WAYNE

I don't have much option do I.

TOM

Perhaps this is a better way to be, it could save your life one day, you never know.

WAYNE

What do you mean.

TOM

Oh nothing, Wayne, nothing.

EVERYONE COMES BACK TO THEIR PLACES IN THE COURTROOM, JACK ENTERS.

TOM

Be upstanding.

JACK

Well, where do I start in summing up the evidence we've heard today. We have seen the innocent young Wayne enjoying what appears to be an idyllic childhood, a happy and contented child. How could we have then progressed to the Wayne we see before us today, wasting his chances of education, being excluded from school. Petty crime leading to serious drug dealing and terrorising his estate, finally responsibility for the horrific suicide of a mother and her young daughter. From where I'm seeing this young man, you seem to have made a pretty awful mess of your life What we have to decide, or perhaps, what you have to decide is if you want to get out of this mess, if you are willing to change for the better. You're attitude to this court will be the thing that ultimately decides your fate. Unfortunately from what I've seen you seem very unlikely to change your ways. Therefore I feel I have no option but to direct the jury to find you guilty.

WAYNE

Change my ways, change my ways, you fucking idiot. How can I change my ways.

JACK

You obviously can't Wayne, which leaves me no option but to declare that you Wayne Bailey have been found guilty and all I can do now is declare the sentence.

This court takes a very dim view of your heinous behaviour culminating in the sad death of a mother and her young daughter. We also take the view that justice should be an eye for an eye and therefore find only one sentence suitable. That is, you shall be hung by the neck until dead, and may God have mercy upon your soul.

THE SIDES OF THE DOCK DROP DOWN AND A ROPE WITH A HANGMANS NOOSE DROPS FROM THE CEILING.

WAYNE STANDS IN SHOCK.

WAYNE

What the fuck.

TOM PLACES A BLACK HOOD OVER WAYNES HEAD AND PUTS THE NOOSE ROUND HIS NECK.

NOW ALL IN SLOW MOTION.

CUT TO CLOSE UP OF WAYNES HEAD AS HE SCREAMS OUT.

WAYNE

No.

CUT TO THE TRAP DOOR OPENING.

CUT TO SLIGHTLY WIDER SHOT OF WAYNE AS HE FALLS OUT OF SHOT.

CUT TO WIDE SHOT OF WAYNE STANDING UP TO HIS KNEES IN THE TRAPDOOR.

WAYNES SCREAMING GRADUALLY DECLINES AS HE REALISES HE'S STANDING AND ISN'T DEAD.

WAYNE

I'm sorry, I'm sorry, please I don't want to die. Anything, I'll do anything.

JACK

That's more like it Wayne.

JACK AND TOM RELEASE WAYNE AND SIT HIM IN THE CHAIR. HE IS VISIBLY SHOCKED.

BRENDA COMES WITH A CUP OF TEA AND HANDS IT TO WAYNE.

BRENDA

Tea, Wayne.

WAYNE

Thanks.

BRENDA

I'm sorry we had to do this to you Wayne but we couldn't see another way. I'm a social worker and we've arranged for you to go to a safe house before you're re housed. There are people out there to help you.

TOM

No, no, I thought I could do this your way, but I can't, I'm sorry. I've tried it your way, now it's my turn. I've just done my tour in Afghanistan, my mates have died out there to keep little shits like you safe to roam the streets terrorising people. You're going to give him a new flat, a new start, I've got mates who've lost arms and legs who get nothing. They have to fight for compensation for basic necessities it's not right. I've got a confession for you all, I'm not Sergeant Tom Higgins, I lied. My real name is Sergeant John Edge and my mother was Maureen Edge and my little sister was Vicky. That's right Wayne you were responsible for the death of my mother and my sweet baby sister.

112

HE PULLS OUT A GUN AND AIMS IT AT WAYNE'S HEAD.

TOM

I can't forgive you for that.

HE MOVES CLOSER TO WAYNE AND SHOOTS HIM IN THE HEAD.

BRENDA AND DIANE SCREAM.

JACK

Oh fuck.

TOM FALLS TO HIS KNEES, CRYING.

TOM

Real life doesn't have happy endings.

HE PUTS THE GUN IN HIS MOUTH AND PULLS THE TRIGGER.

FADE TO BLACK.

DULCE ET DECORUM
EST PRO PATRIA MORI

Narrator.

I said to my dad recently, what's all this fuss about the First World war, I mean, it was ninety years ago. He said ninety years isn't that long ago, his dads', dad was in it, and millions of young boys just like me.

Private John Parr.

It doesn't seem that long ago to me either. I'm Private John Parr and I was the first British soldier killed in the war. I must say I wasn't expecting to die when I signed up, I thought it was going to be a grand adventure, it was all supposed to be over by Christmas. It says on my gravestone that I was twenty but it's not true, I was sixteen, I lied. I wasn't the only one who lied, it was a fairly common practice. I left my job as a golf caddy to become a bicycle scout with the Middlesex Regiment. I was shot and killed near Mons on 21st August 1914 while scouting on my bicycle. My war lasted less than one day.

Narrator.

It surprised me when I found out they had a fantastic postal service in those days and men would regularly write home. Here is part of a letter written by Private Jack Mudd, four days before he was killed taking part in the third battle of Ypres, known as Passchendaele. He was only thirty one when he left his wife Lizzie and their children to go to war.

Private Jack Mudd.

The ground conditions today are atrocious, many men are up to their knees in slimy clinging mud. Some times it is so bad they would slip under and literally drown. Their cries for help will haunt me for the rest of my life, but we have been instructed that when attacking on no account should we stop to help our fallen comrades. It is my worst nightmare that I should die in that awful slimy swamp. I think of you constantly love, I often take your photo out of my pocket and look at your dear face and think of the times we have had together, some lovely days eh love. When I think again of some of the worry I have caused you it makes me all the more eager to get home to you to atone for all the worry and anxious moments you have to put up with.

Narrator.

In November Lizzie received a copy of Army Form B 104-83 telling her Jack had been posted missing. His nightmare had come true, his body was never recovered.

Rev Cyril Lomax

I'm Reverend Cyril Lomax. I graduated in History from Oxford and was ordained in 1895. I didn't enter the war immediately as I had a commitment to my parish and had to remain in Blighty, but I joined the Durham Light Infantry in July 1916. As a rule I am a brute about letter writing, but not out here, things are so different. One is so glad to receive a letter. You can have no idea how one longs for the post and how disappointed one feels if there is nothing for one. Everybody hates the mud, but we bathe in it, wade in it, sleep in it. Clods of it adorn the most secret recesses of ones clothes, books and papers. I draw for my amusement and my sanity, although I do censor some of my drawings. If I wanted to make you creep I might have put a realistic foreground of dead Bosch and our own, fallen in every sort of attitude; some half buried by shells, others in the open. But the reality is too ghastly. There is none of the dignity of death the flies and the rats see to that. The impression left up upon one is, one of waste. Indeed the whole country would admirably do as a picture of the material conditions of Hell.

Narrator

It's hard to believe that three million men volunteered to serve in the British Army in the first two years of the war, but there were so many dead and injured the Government had to introduce conscription. All men between the age of nineteen and not yet forty would have to serve. Amazingly the 1916 Military Service Act contained categories which were exempt. Clause D stated ; exemption on the grounds of a conscientious objection to the undertaking of combative service. Sixteen thousand men applied for exemption. Albert Brockelsby was one of them, he was a Methodist and a devout Christian. When asked to preach a sermon at his local church this is what he said.

Albert Brockelsby.

Can you imagine Christ dressed in army uniform, armed with a machine gun, or bayoneting a German soldier. That picture is impossible and we all know it. My family received a white feather, the sign of cowardice, but they stood by me. I was arrested and put in prison where I kept my spirits up by praying and singing hymns. Along with other objectors I was taken to France and before hundreds of other soldiers we were sentenced to death. I had never felt the need of my God more than in that moment. Thank God my prayers were answered and none of us were actually executed, we were sent to a work camp to serve hard labour. Seventy three objectors died as a result of their punishment. In the House of Commons Captain Stephen Gynne MP said. There is one thing that nobody can deny them, that is courage. The most difficult form of courage in the world; the courage of the individual against the crowd. It made us feel we were not alone.

Pte Ronald Scurf.

I'm Private Ronald Scurf and I knew that to fight was the right thing, after all, the Chaplain told me so. I am an Artillery Observer, it was my job to locate and target the enemy positions. On the 7th June 1917 at ten past three in the morning army sappers detonated ninety one thousand tons of high explosive placed under the German front line. It was only one of nineteen other massive explosions along the seven mile front. The explosion could be heard over one hundred miles away in London. For fourteen hours shells blasted the German positions, can you imagine the Hell those poor fellows must have gone through. I was sent into No Mans Land and I can't describe the shapes and colours human bodies can take when they're blown to smithereens . I came across a young German sitting holding a photo, at first I thought he was alive as there was no outward sign that he was in fact dead. The photo looked like my wife and I felt sick with shame. That was when I made a private pact with God never to harm another person again. I tried to join the Ambulance Brigade but they wouldn't let me, so from that moment on whenever I was aiming the guns I always made sure they would miss. I never told anyone what I was doing , I could have been hung for it On the first day of the Somme there were sixty thousand casualties; one third of them were killed, but later on the tactics changed with the use of more gas attacks, for they had realised that a casualty was more of a drain on resources than a dead man. We thought it was important to bury the dead although the French didn't bother so much. One we didn't bury was a hand which was left sticking out of the mud. It was known as Farewell Freddie's Hand and was touched for good luck as the men passed to go over the top.

Narrator.

It's hard to believe now that they could use such awful stuff on fellow human beings but this is what some of the men said about the gas attacks. First Bombardier Palmer.

Bombardier Palmer.

The faces of our lads who lay in the open changed colour and presented a gruesome spectacle. Their faces and hands gradually assumed a blue and green colour and their buttons and metal fittings on their uniforms were all discoloured. Many lay there with their legs drawn up and clutching their throats.

Narrator.

And Lance Sergeant Elmer Cotton.

Sgt Elmer Cotton.

Propped up against a wall was a dozen, all gassed, their colours were black, green and blue, their tongues hanging out and eyes staring. One or two were dead and others beyond human aid, some were coughing up green froth from their lungs. As we advanced we passed many more men lying in the ditches and gutterways, shells were bursting all around. My respirator fell to pieces with the continual removal and readjustment, the gas closed my eyes and filled them with matter and I could not see. I was left lying in the trench with one other gassed man and various wounded beings and corpses and forced to lie and spit, cough and gasp the whole of the day in that awful place.

Narrator.

Also Lance Corporal Abraham

Lce Cpl Abraham.

Although our road was only slightly sunken it lay at the foot of a gentle slope and thus acted as a gas trap. Our Colonel and

Medical Officer had both been affected by the stuff and during the morning they were carried away on stretchers. The rest of us stayed out there all day, coughing and retching and gradually going blind.

Narrator.

And on the frightening night patrols. Second Lieutenant Cooper.

Snd Lt Cooper.

I really believe that I am after all a coward for I don't like patrolling. Just last week the battalion who alternate with us here lost three Officers and an NCO on this business in front of my trenches.

Let me try to picture what it is like. I am asked to take out an officers patrol of seven men. Our duties; to get out to the German listening post, wait for their patrol and scupper it. I choose my favourite corporal, a gentleman, a commercial traveller for the Midland Educational in civilian life and my six most intelligent and courageous men.

All sentries are informed we are going out so we shan't be fired on. Magazines are charged to the full, one round in the breech: bayonets ready; my revolver is nicely oiled.

Everything is ready. As soon as the dusk is sufficiently dark, we get out into the front of the trenches by climbing up on to the parapet and tumbling over as rapidly as possible so as not to be silhouetted against the last traces of the sunset. Out we walk through the barbed wire entanglement zone through which an approaching enemy must climb. But we have a zigzag path through the thirty yards or so of prickly unpleasantness; this path is only known to a few. The night has become horribly dark already.

We wriggle along through the long grass for a hundred yards or so and lie and wait and listen. In the German trenches we hear the faint hum of conversation. Nothing is to be heard near us, but there is a very ominous sign. No shots are being fired from the trenches in front of us, no flares are being sent up and there is no working party out. This points to only one thing and that is that they also have a patrol out. There is no other conclusion.

Suddenly quite close to the corporal and myself there is a heavy rustling in the long grass on the right. Now, if ever before I know the meaning of fear. My heart thumps so heavily that they surely must hear it, my face is covered with cold perspiration, my revolver goes back with a sharp click and my hand trembles. I have no inclination to run away, quite the reverse, but I have one solitary thought; I am going to kill a man.

This I repeat over and over again and the thought makes me miserable and at the same time joyful for I shall have accounted for one of the blackguards even if I go myself. Then quite abruptly they change their direction and make off to the right where to follow them would be courting certain disaster. So with great caution we come in and breathe again. When we are safely inside the trench, I sit down and cry uncontrollably.

There were moments of sanity though. On Christmas Day 1914 only five months into the war the German, French and British troops disobeyed superiors and fraternized with the enemy along two thirds of the front. This, in a time of war was punishable by death. We sang Christmas carols, exchanged photos of loved ones, shared rations and played football. Generals on both sides declared this act treasonable and subject to courts martial. By March 1915 the fraternizing movement had been eradicated and the killing machine was put back in full operation. Our moment of sanity was over.

Narrator.

How wonderful it must have been for a son to receive a letter from his mother to keep him sane in all that carnage. Mrs Cooper Clarke wrote regularly to hers.

Mrs Cooper Clarke

My darling, we are so glad to hear from you. Although your notes contain so little news they convey to us what we chiefly want to know, that you are safe. My letter was returned to me with 'missing' written in red ink across the front of the envelope. Although this was standard procedure, it was a dreadful shock when it arrived. I couldn't bring myself to accept he may be gone he was only eighteen when he joined as a rifleman, he was just a boy. I was desperate to find some news of him, and wrote to The Rifle Corps, The Red Cross and finally The War Office, all to no avail. Finally in July I received confirmation that he had died of dysentery in a German field hospital. My darling boy was dead.

Narrator.

Other women like Joan Williams wanted to help the war by working in a munitions factory in Chiswick. Her decision was very unusual as she was upper class and was more used to people working for her.

Joan Williams

My parents were not at all keen when I told them I was going to work in the factory, but I stuck to my guns. I was afraid the men would be jealous of the women doing skilled work but was surprised that I experienced no problems in that regard. I worked on a seven foot Drummond lathe and took great pride in my work. Over a period of time I got to know other girls who worked in the munitions factory and dealt with the explosive TNT. Their bravery I felt was most admirable. I was less impressed with some of the language of my fellow workers and attempted to improve their vocabulary to curtail the swearing. When I finished at the factory I was presented with a tortoiseshell inkpot which surprised and touched me.

Narrator.

Amazingly in 1916 they were running out of troops again so the Millitary Service Bill was extended to include married men. Men like Private Mowbray Meades who was thirty five and very surprised to find himself in active service. He wrote to his wife.

Pte Mowbray Meades.

Well, dearest, I know you have been thinking a good deal about me today and wondering how I have faired. I thought about you all last evening and pictured what we should have been doing, listening to the bells ringing in Christmas morning. When I awoke this morning my first thoughts were of you and our dear little girls, and I fancied I could see them running down to get their stockings. Well dears I can say I had the finest dinner I've had in the army. We had roast pork, potatoes and cabbage, fig pudding, jam roll, Christmas pudding and jelly. Of course it was all of our own procuring and not Army rations.

Narrator.

I hope he enjoyed his lunch as he was soon wounded, seriously enough to be sent home. He recuperated in Bradford where he wrote home.

Pte Mowbray Meades.

I wish there was some sign of an early finish to the war and no such possibility of my again returning, but we shall have to prepare ourselves for such an eventuality. The days when we were convinced that the war would be over by Christmas are long gone. I know I am not in proper shape to go back to the front but fear I will have to go.

Narrator.

Mowbray was sent back to the Front before the first of the great German offences of 1919 when he was taken prisoner. His wife received a letter from the Agence des Prisonnieres de Guerre telling her that her husband had died in the Millitary Hospital at Lille of inflammation of the lungs. How sad that they sent him back to the front.

Of the less wanted Christmas presents, Private Archie Surfleet wrote about lice.

Pte Archie Surfleet.

If you're nearly frozen, they keep quiet. As soon as you warm up the blasted lice start to bite like the devil. It's horrible, I often think it's one of the worst things we have to endure out here.

Narrator.

At the outbreak of war an extraordinary black man named Walter Tull volunteered. He was born in Folkstone, but his father was from Barbados and his mother was a local girl, they had six children together. Sadly his mother died when he was just seven and his father re married only to die himself two years later His stepmother wasn't able to cope with all six children so Walter and his brother Edward were sent to a Methodist orphanage in Bethnal Green. After finishing school he was apprenticed as a printer but was always a talented footballer. He progressed through the amateur leagues to play for the First Division Club, Tottenham Hotspur, at a time when this was unheard of for a black man. Walter was obviously a very strong character as he had to endure racist taunts every time he played. He joined the Football Battalion, one of the pals battalions formed to encourage football supporters to follow suite. They soon realised his leadership abilities and he was promoted to Sergeant. In July 1916 he took part in the major Somme offensive after which he was found to be suffering from 'acute mania', a condition now known as post traumatic stress disorder. He was sent home to recuperate during which time he was recommended for officer training. This was an unprecedented decision as Army regulations forbade black people from becoming officers. He must have been exceedingly well thought of by his superiors.

Lieutenant Walter Tull, now the first black officer in the British Army was sent to Italy where he was Mentioned in Dispatches by Major General Sydney Lawford.

Gen Sydney Lawford

For gallantry and coolness while leading his company of twenty six men on a raiding party , to cross the River Piave into enemy territory and bringing them all back unharmed it is recommended he receive the Military Cross.

Narrator.

Later he returned to Northern France where he was shot in the neck and killed in an action near the village of Favreuil. He was such a popular officer that many valliant attempts were made by his men to retrieve his body while still under fire. Sadly despite their efforts his body was never found.

Narrator.

During the course of the war there were many soldiers who wrote poetry to express their feelings, Rupert Brooke was one of them. He was commissioned into the Royal Naval Division and when sailing for the Dardanelles he developed septicaemia from a mosquito bite.

He died on a hospital ship off the Greek island of Skyros and was buried in an olive grove on the island. It's strangely ironic that he should be buried in such a beautiful place when he died taking part in such an obscene war. His poetry was very optimistic in the early days of the war, here is a brief excerpt of one of them.

Rupert Brooke.

If I should die, think only this of me; That there's some corner of a foreign field That is for ever England.

Narrator.

Later on in the war the sentiment changed completely and some poets like Seigfried Sassoon even published articles in the Times condemning the war.

Seigfried Sasoon.

Early in the war my brother, Hamo was mortally wounded at Gallipoli, I was devastated and took unnecessary risks trying to avenge his death, but I didn't care if I lived or died. They even awarded me the Military Cross in 1916. Were it not for the intervention of my dear friend Robert Graves I would have been up for Courts Martial for my article condemning the war. I could have been hung but Robert managed to convince the review board I was suffering from shell shock. I was sent for treatment to Craiglockhart Hospital in Edinburgh where I met another poet Wilfred Owen. Dear God, Craiglockhart was a fearful place, almost as bad the front itself. Most of the men there were shadows of the people they once were. The early treatment consisted of nothing better than barking orders at them accusing them of cowardice and malingering. Later on they introduced electric shock treatment, a truly barbaric process. The vast majority of the men were completely incapacitated by severe shaking making them unable to walk or complete the simplest of tasks. Whenever there was a loud or sudden noise these poor souls would fling themselves to the floor or under a bed, many would have urinated or defecated. It was some time before a more caring treatment regime was introduced. I don't think I could have endured it had it not been for my friendship with Wilfred Owen After treatment I was returned to active service, first in Palestine and later in France where I was wounded. Once again I was sent home to England where thank God, I took no further part in the war.

Narrator.

In January1917 Wilfred Owen was posted to France, his first action was to hold a dug out in no mans land for fifty hours whilst under heavy shelling. He suffered concussion in March but was returned to the front line in April. He wrote to his mother.

Wilfred Owen.

My own dearest mother. Immediately after I sent my last letter we were rushed up into the line. Twice in one day we went over the top, gaining both our objectives.

Our Company led the attack and of course lost a certain number of men. I had some extraordinary escapes from shells and bullets. Fortunately there was no bayonet work, since the Hun ran before we got up to his trench. Never before has the Battalion encountered such intense shelling as rained on us as we advanced in the open.

The next day Lieutenant Colonel Luxmore sent round this message.

I was filled with admiration at the conduct of the Battalion under heavy shell fire. The leadership of the officers was excellent and the conduct of the men beyond praise. The reward we got for this was to remain in the line for twelve more days.

For twelve days I did not wash my face, nor take off my boots, nor sleep a deep sleep. For twelve days we lay in holes, where at any moment a shell might put us out. I think the worst incident was one wet night when we lay up against a railway embankment. A big shell lit on the top of the bank just two yards from my head and blew me into the air. I passed the following days in a hole just big enough to lie in and covered with corrugated iron. Another officer lay opposite in a similar hole covered with earth. I think the terribly long time we stayed unrelieved was unavoidable; yet it makes us feel bitterly towards those in England who might relieve us, and will not.

126

In August 1918 whilst being treated for shell shock he wrote some of his most creative work. He was returned to active service in France and was awarded the Military Cross for bravery at Armiens. Tragically he was killed on the 4th November whilst trying to lead his men across the Sambre Canal at Ors.

This was just one week from the end of the War, which ended on 11th November at eleven o'clock in the morning. The last British soldier to die was Private George Ellison a regular soldier who had been in the army before the war started.

It is so tragic that men were forced to fight right up to the end. George was shot and killed while scouting the outskirts of the Belgian town of Mons with just over one hour left to go. It is ironic that his resting place in the St Symphorien cemetery near Mons is on the opposite side of the path, just a few steps, from Private John Parr the first British casualty. The number of casualties both military and civilian was about forty million; nineteen million dead and twenty one million wounded.

The futility of it all is expressed in Wilfred Owens' poem..

Wilfred Owen.

Bent double, like old beggars under sacks, Knock-kneed, coughing like hags, we cursed through sludge, Till on haunting flares we turned our backs And towards our distant rest began to trudge. Men marched asleep. Many had lost their boots But limped on, blood shot. All went lame; all blind; Drunk with fatigue; deaf even to the hoots Of tired, outstripped Five- Nines that dropped behind.

Gas! Gas! Quick boys! An ecstasy of fumbling, Fitting the clumsy helmets just in time; But someone still was yelling out and stumbling, And flound'ring like a man in fire or lime... Dim' through misty panes and thick green light, As under a green sea, I saw him drowning. In all my dreams, before my helpless sight, He plunges at me, guttering, choking, drowning.

If in some smothering dreams you too could pace Behind the wagon that we flung him in, And watch the white eyes writhing in his face, His hanging face, like a devil's sick of sin; If you could hear, at every jolt, the blood Come gargling from the froth-corrupted lungs, Obscene as cancer, bitter as the cud Of vile, incurable sores on innocent tongues, My friend, you would not tell with such high zest To children ardent for some desperate glory, The old Lie; Dulce et Decorum est Pro patria mori.

CONFESSION

A MONOLOGUE

I'm just about to leave my husband, I've had enough; this is the letter I've left for him.

Dear Tony,

I don't know how to say this, well yes I do. In short I'm leaving you. God knows why I didn't do it years ago, but I suppose I never had the guts. I'm sorry but you were always such a bully and I've finally had enough. Even now I'm still apologising, I must get out of the habit of doing that. Wendy told me to stop apologising and she's right, oh you remember Wendy, she's the tall red head who's just joined the choir. Not that I expect you to have noticed, you were always so wrapped up in your own self importance. Taking confession, always being so supercilious, well I've got a surprise for you, I've a confession for you. Wendy is my lover and you drove me to her. I cannot tell you how much I love her, she's kind, gentle and caring, in fact all the things you were unable to be. The last thing I expected was to fall in love with a woman, in fact I'm sure you can find something in your wretched Bible that says it's a sin, well guess what, I don't give a damn. Believe me a multiple orgasm with Wendy is worth a lifetime in hell. Well that's it I've nothing else to say.

Goodbye, yours Maureen.

RONALD'S WAR.

A MONOLOGUE.

I bought my Austin Seven brand new in 1935, well I say I bought her, it was actually Doreen who paid for her, she'd come into a legacy from her Auntie Maud.

She was a bit of a character Auntie Maud, none of the rest of the family had anything to do with her, which is why I suppose Doreen got the money.

She always used to say, just because she lives with Amelia doesn't mean there's any hanky panky going on, and even if there is, so what, judge ye not lest ye yourself be judged.

She was like that, always looking for the good in anyone, you'll get your reward in heaven, she'd say, although in our case we got our reward from heaven, good old Auntie Maud.

We even lashed out the extra seven pounds for the deluxe with the sun roof, Doreen said, it will be easier for Auntie to look down and see us.

We certainly had some fun in her, picnics in the country, trips to the sea side and unlike our bicycles we didn't get wet when it rained, although Doreen made us keep the roof open whenever possible just in case Auntie was looking, I think they were probably the best years of my life.

We were so lucky, I got promoted to senior officer at the station which pleased Doreen, she always worried when I was working, it meant more responsibility but less front line fire fighting, which I missed a little.

Life for us was blissfully happy for almost four years, in fact looking back, those carefree years before the war were good for everyone, not just us.

We could all see it coming but didn't want to admit it, and of course the, peace for our time speech made us cling to the hope of a negotiated peace, it wasn't to be of course, but even the early years of the war lulled us into a false sense of security as nothing much happened.

I think as a nation we are good at pulling together when the chips are down, even so we hadn't expected what a devastating effect modern warfare would have.

People were very surprised and frankly very scared when the war came to us, last time it was all over seas, I remember thinking when I laid up the car, I hope we're all here to use her when this mess is over.

I'd taken the spark plugs out and put oil down the bores and turned her over every week to stop her seizing up, even though I couldn't use her I kept her ready, just in case.

When I was a lad I'd worked in a garage before joining the fire brigade, so I had been taught to respect motors and to treat them properly.

One of my greatest pleasures was to work on an Austin Ulster that raced at Brooklands, not that I was allowed to do anything too crucial and when Mr Gordon won his class we all felt immense pride and that some small part of his victory was because of us.

When the war first started I thought I was so lucky not to be called up, I know fireman is not the safest job, but at least I was at home with Doreen and the kids.

I'd sometimes talk to my father about his war but he didn't like to talk about it, he was in the cavalry, he used to ride the gun carriages.

He told me how he removed his spurs and replaced them with halfpennies so he wouldn't hurt the horses, an amazing thing to have done in all that carnage, but I have to admit I'd probably have done the same.

I knew Doreen always used to worry about me when I was at work, but as the war went on it was me who had to worry about her, she'd got a job at the munitions factory, I didn't want her to, but as she said, everyone has to do their bit and this bit is mine.

Of course so many men had been called up we had to use the women, in fact without the land army girls, the ambulance women and the factory girls and all the others we couldn't have kept going.

Then the blitz on London started and we were all in the front line, with nowhere to hide, for eleven weeks day or night the bombing was ceaseless, there was no let up we were working as long as we were able to stand, I didn't go home from work for days at a time.

So many bombs and incendiaries fell that many nights our worst fear was realised, the fire storm, you could sense it coming, first a gentle breeze, then the wind, then that extraordinary roaring sound and the unbearable heat.

133

When a fire storm took hold there was nothing you could do except let it burn itself out and prey you didn't get trapped in the inferno, or crushed by the falling buildings.

After a while we got used to the noise a building would make before it collapsed, an odd creaking sound, but with all the other noise going on you couldn't always hear it and sadly many men were crushed to death this way.

There was one night in December 1940 when the Luftwaffe dropped so many incendiaries that the whole of the Square Mile was ablaze.

We were getting water from the Thames but it was low tide and even that ran out, some parts of Moorgate were left to burn and then we got the call from Mr Churchill to save Saint Pauls at any cost.

Amazingly it was only hit by one small incendiary bomb which was put out by a fire watcher with a bucket of sand, all around was ablaze but Saint Pauls was untouched.

I think initially a hell of a lot of people were scared to death by what was going on, but it's amazing how quickly you become hardened to such things, you have to or you don't survive.

Even during all this madness people still went out to enjoy themselves, dancing the night away in underground clubs, going to the flicks or the pub. I was told the Savoy still kept it's policy of only permitting dancing for people in evening dress which I felt was unfair on the troops on leave who couldn't dance as they were in uniform.

We'd become used to seeing casualties from the front and relatives dead or missing, but innocent children were much harder to bear and sadly at work I was seeing far too many, even though lots of them had been evacuated to the country.

I'll always remember Jack who I went to school with, he volunteered for the navy right from the start.

When he came home on leave we met up for a drink, he told me his wife was pregnant but it couldn't have been his, he swore me to secrecy, then I heard he'd volunteered for submarines, I can't imagine how anyone can go in those things.

I couldn't meet him on his next leave but I heard he was in a bad way, they said he'd been mined on two separate occasions, he was in such a state his mother wouldn't let him go back when his leave expired.

The next day the Military Police came for him, but his mother said, I am keeping him for one more week and then you can have him back, surprisingly enough they went away, of course they came back a few days later, then five weeks after that we heard the news he was killed in action.

His mother stood by his wife regardless of the tittle tattle, and when the child was born she was still there, it's people like that who win wars.

Work was tough but Jacks' mother was always an inspiration to me and when London's burning someone has to deal with it.

You almost couldn't cope with it, not just the physical effort but the mental effort needed to turn out night after night knowing what you have to face.

Then all of a sudden the raids stopped, day and night, and for me it was almost back to normal, the only bad news was the retreat from Dunkirk, I lost my cousin there and his brother only just got out although he lost a leg, such a shame as he had been a promising athlete.

Tom told me they were on the beach together for three days before they had a chance to escape, all the time strafed by machine gun and rocket fire from the Luftwaffe.

Hundreds of small boats had been commandeered to transfer the troops from the beach to the larger ships, mostly crewed by the navy though some were taken over by their owners, fishermen and the like.

The first one Tom and Harry were on was destroyed so they had to swim back to shore for another miserable day sheltering as best they could waiting for another chance to get away.

Tom said the last time he saw Harry he was boarding a London tug and assumed he would get home safely, it was only when he got back he found out it was sunk on the way.

His last attempt to leave was on a fishing boat but once again it was strafed by machine gun fire which destroyed his leg, and he was incredibly lucky to have got out on one of the last hospital ships.

We were grateful to have only lost Harry, although I don't think Tom saw it that way.

The medical advances in those days were amazing, they gave him a new tin leg, but I heard later he'd been killed in a tragic accident, apparently he fell under a tube train and was killed instantly.

I hope that was it, but I just think the thought of not being able to run ever again was too much for him, war makes people do crazy things, sometimes they end up heroes and sometimes they don't.

Still in all this madness normal life did carry on, Doreen and I went to the Odeon whenever we could and even went to the Palladium once, we saw Tommy Trinder, Arther Askey, a full bill and the dancers, that was a night to remember.

We had some more nights, and days to remember when the Doodle Bugs started to come over, the papers said they were rocket powered bombs launched from France.

The scariest thing about them was you could hear them coming, a strange sort of wurr,wurr, noise that would suddenly stop, that was the frightening thing, when the noise stopped it meant they had run out of fuel and they were coming down.

It was alright if they did it above your head as they would glide past you to the ground but if it was coming towards you and stopped that's when you were in trouble.

As the war went on the RAF got faster planes and would intercept them and shoot them down or sometimes fly alongside them and flip them with their wing tips into the Kent countryside where no one was injured.

Eventually even the doodle bugs stopped and life became a bit more relaxed, people still lost friends and relatives overseas but at home the worst gripe was about the rationing, it was odd that there were children who had never seen a banana.

I managed to buy some petrol on the black market but was too scared to use it as it was for the forces and marked with a dye, but I promised myself as soon as it was over I would take a chance and go for a run in the car.

We plodded on with more and more good news, then all of a sudden it was all over,

Victory in Europe was declared and although it seemed a long time afterwards we eventually got Victory in Japan and the whole thing really was over.

Even though we still had rationing everyone organised street parties to celebrate with tables in the street and bunting, what gay times we had, getting back to normal was almost an anti-climax.

Doreen gave up her job at the factory although a lot of the girls didn't, which did cause a bit of resentment from some of the returning chaps, but things had changed, everyones lives had changed and we had to move on and look to the future.

What times we'd been through both physically and emotionally, but we'd all come through it, that's what mattered, I always felt grateful especially at work, every bombed out house or building told a tale of someone who didn't make it.

Everything in the garden was wonderful, things couldn't be better, then one day at work I got a phone call to say Doreen had been taken ill, no details but I was to get home as soon as possible.

When I got there her mother met me at the door, it's bad news Ron, she said, Doreens dead, I'm afraid I just went to pieces I couldn't accept it, how could we have gone through all that for nothing, it seemed so dreadfully unfair.

Apparently she'd had a massive heart attack, no warning, nothing, just taken from me in an instant, I sobbed like a child.

I'm afraid I embarrassed myself at the funeral, I broke down at the graveside and wept, I know I should have had more self control but I couldn't help myself.

The kids are at Doreens mums, I couldn't look after myself, let alone them, I would cry uncontrollably for no reason, I felt so utterly helpless.

When I woke this morning I knew what I was going to do, I just wanted one last drive in the car first, I hadn't been able to in the war and anyway I had to warm the engine, I didn't want it to stall half way through.

It should be easy, just put the hose on the exhaust pipe and the other end through the window, off you go to sleep, easy as that, all the pains gone.

It was raining when I went out, a terrible day, so I was surprised when I got to Audley Wood it stopped raining, the sun came out and there was the most amazing rainbow.

I couldn't see it properly until I opened the sun roof, it was so beautiful I started crying, but not in the same way as before, somehow in that moment I'd let everything go, I knew Doreen was up there looking down, and I felt peace.

I threw the pipe away and drove back like a lunatic to get the kids, it's such a lovely day, I think we should have a picnic.

MURDER AT WESTHAMPNETT HOUSE

A MURDER MYSTERY.

CAST LIST, IN ORDER OF APPEARANCE.

SCROTUM, THE BUTLER.

GEORGINA ARCHER, ACCOUNTANT.

SQUADRON LEADER THOMAS DASHFOOT CHURCH.

NED MELLORS, GARDEN DESIGNER.

EDNA SEACOLE, NURSE.

AMANDA BLOOM, CATERER.

LADY ANITA DASHFOOT CHURCH.

REVEREND FLOWERDEW.

LORD ANTHONY DASHFOOT CHURCH.

INSPECTOR

MURDER AT WESTHAMPNETT HOUSE

AN OLD STYLE COUNTRY
HOUSE BELL RINGS AND
THE FRONT DOOR OPENS

SCROTUM

Good afternoon madam, I'm Scrotum the butler and how may I help you.

GEORGINA

Oh, good afternoon Scrotum, I'm Georgina Archer, I'm here for the meeting with Lord Dashfoot Church.

SCROTUM

Yes madam, you're the first to arrive, if you come this way there are refreshments laid on in the dining room.

FOOTSTEPS

Lord Anthony's brother Thomas will look after you until the others arrive.

THE DINING ROOM DOOR OPENS

SCROTUM

Good afternoon Sir, this is Georgina Archer.

THOMAS

Thank you Scrotum. Hello my dear can I get you a drink, I'm just having a gin and tonic and what's your poison.

GEORGINA

Well I don't usually drink at this time of day.

THOMAS

I'm sure the sun is well over the yardarm now dearie, how about a glass of white wine.

GEORGINA

Alright then, perhaps just a small one.

CLINKING GLASSES

THOMAS

Here we are my dear.

GEORGINA

Thank you, but that's rather on the large size for me.

THOMAS

Nonsense my dear, it will put some colour in your cheeks. Now then Georgina and what does a pretty filly like you do.

GEORGINA

Well actually I'm an accountant.

THOMAS

I say, smashing, a good figure and good at figures.

Myself I'm Squadron Leader down the road at Westhampnett airfield and are you spoken for my dear.

THE DOOR BELL RINGS

GEORGINA

I wonder who else is coming to the meeting.

THOMAS

You didn't answer my question, are you available my dear.

GEORGINA

I don't have a relationship at the moment I'm rather busy with my career.

THE DINING ROOM DOOR OPENS

SCROTUM

Ned Mellors and Edna Seacole.

THOMAS

Thank you Scrotum. I'm Squadron Leader Thomas Dashfoot Church, Lord Anthonys brother and this rather splendid filly is

Georgina Archer and she's an accountant don't you know.

NED

I'm Ned Mellors and this is Edna Seacole, we met on the train on the way down, I'm a garden designer and Edna is a nurse.

THOMAS

Drinks anyone.

EDNA

Scotch please, it was a damn long way down here on a train with no bar.

THOMAS

Well done old girl, I don't have to ask if you want sippers or gulpers. That's a large scotch, and what can

I get for you young man.

NED

Do you have a beer please.

CLINKING GLASSES

THOMAS

Yes I'm sure we do. I think I'll have a top up myself, here we go, bottoms up.

EDNA

Thanks, my stomach was thinking my throat had been cut.

THOMAS

Top hole, I'll bash out another couple of gulpers for us, shall I.

EDNA

Seems silly not to.

THOMAS

Bang on old thing, I like a gal who can hold her liquor.

THE DOOR BELL RINGS

There are some sandwiches here if anyone wants to partake, I'm more of a liquid lunch man myself but don't hold back yourselves if you fancy a nibble.

THE DINING ROOM DOOR OPENS

SCROTUM

Amanda Bloom.

THOMAS

Thank you Scrotum. Come in my dear, join the party, can I get you a drink.

AMANDA

Just an orange juice, please, I'm working later and I like to remain sober when I'm working.

THOMAS

My dear, you're far too attractive to have to work, some chap should have snapped you up by now.

AMANDA

Surprisingly I choose to work, it's my company doing the catering today, did you not notice my bagels.

THE DOOR BELL RINGS

THOMAS

I did actually, it's the first thing I noticed when you entered the room.

AMANDA

No, I meant the food.

THOMAS

Oh, so did I my dear, so did I.

THE DINING ROOM DOOR OPENS

LADY ANITA

Hello everyone. For those of you who don't know me I'm Lady Anita, Lord Anthony's wife and this is Reverend Robert Flowerdew. Please make yourselves at home, Anthony is busy at the moment but he won't be too long.

THOMAS

In the mean time I suggest a drink, what will it be Reverend.

REVEREND FLOWERDEW

Thank you, perhaps I might push the boat out with a small sherry

THOMAS

We don't do small here Reverend, I'm sure I've a decent sized schooner here somewhere. Yes here we are.

CLINKING GLASSES

REVEREND FLOWERDEW

Thanks awfully, but I don't want to end up squiffy, I don't usually drink as a rule.

LADY ANITA

You don't have to drink it all Reverend, just have a sip. I'm sorry Thomas does have a somewhat forthright manner when it comes to alcohol, or anything else come to think of it.

THOMAS

You know you love it old girl.

LADY ANITA

Actually, I don't and please remove your hand from my bottom.

THOMAS

You're such a spoil sport, you know I love a quick grope with you. Got to have something to keep the blood flowing old girl.

LADY ANITA

You really don't get it do you.

THOMAS

Not with you I don't.

REVEREND FLOWERDEW

I'm awfully sorry to interrupt Lady Anita, but I was wondering if you knew why Lord Anthony had asked us here today.

LADY ANITA

I'm afraid I don't Reverend, I assume it's something to do with the estate but I'm sure you'll find out soon enough. I must say your sermon last Sunday was one of your wittiest yet. The story of the voice calling Mark to the mountain top turning out to be a dog with a hair lip was most amusing. Mark, mark.

REVEREND FLOWERDEW

Thank you Lady Anita I always try to find some light entertainment in the encircling gloom.

THE DINING ROOM DOOR OPENS

SCROTUM

Ladies and gentlemen Lord Anthony Dashfoot Church.

LORD ANTHONY

Good afternoon everybody, I'm sorry for keeping you waiting but I had an important meeting with the housekeeper and the upstairs maid which delayed me. We shall be eating later when I hope to be able to discuss with you all matters which are of concern to me. In the meantime you are all welcome to enjoy all the facilities at Westhampnett house and gardens.

THOMAS

Thanks awfully old boy but I'm going to lay down in a dark room, I'm feeling a little fragile

EDNA

I must say you look awful, do you need any help.

THOMAS

Actually old girl I do believe I could do with some assistance.

LORD ANTHONY

I'll help you, we can take him to the library. This way

THE DINING ROOM DOOR OPENS, FOOTSTEPS

Are you alright Thomas old chap, I've never seen you like this before.

THE LIBRARY DOOR OPENS

Sit down here, is there anything we can get you.

THOMAS

Yes, a large port, I'm feeling rather flushed.

CLINKING GLASSES

LORD ANTHONY

Here you are old chap.

EDNA

Well your pulse is a little fast, I think you need to relax a little, perhaps the young ladies got you a little over excited. Take these sleeping pills, I'm sure you'll feel better after a couple of hours sleep

THOMAS

Thank you, both of you, I'm sure you're right.

LORD ANTHONY

Jolly good, thanks Edna, you pop off back to the dining room, I'll just wait a moment until he drops off.

EDNA

Excellent, I could do with another snifter, see you in a moment

FOOTSTEPS,
THE DINING ROOM DOOR OPENS.

LADY ANITA

How is he, is he alright.

EDNA

Yes, I'm sure he'll be as right as nine pence once he's had some sleep. Now who's going to get me a drink.

SCROTUM

Yes madam, another large scotch.

CLINKING GLASSES

EDNA

Thank you Scrotum.

146

GEORGINA

Well I must say the gardens are magnificent, would anyone care for a stroll around the estate.

NED

Yes, I'll come with you, I can show you the maze.

GEORGINA

Splendid, that sounds like fun, bye everyone.

THE FRENCH DOORS OPEN

REVEREND FLOWERDEW

Bye.

AMANDA

Yes, bye.

ANTHONY

Enjoy yourselves.

LADY ANITA

Now, how's dinner progressing.

AMANDA

I haven't been to check yet but my staff are very experienced and I can leave it to them. I will be checking later before we eat Lady Anita.

ANTHONY

Don't put the poor girl under pressure dear, after all this is only her first event for us, I'm sure everything is under control.

EDNA

I must say the gardens here are splendid, is Ned the gardener here.

ANTHONY

No he isn't but my present gardener is due to retire at the end of the year. I'll let you into a little secret, I am considering offering the position to Ned but please don't say anything before the meeting.

EDNA

Well I'm sure he's up to the job he does have a magnificent physique, I know I'd certainly let him dig about in my herbaceous border.

AMANDA

Yes he is rather dishy. Do excuse me I'm just popping out to the kitchen to check on the food, I won't be long.

ANTHONY

Splendid, take your time.

THE DINING ROOM DOOR OPENS

SCROTUM

Can I assist anyone with another drink.

EDNA

Don't mind if I do, I'll have another…

SCROTUM

Large scotch madam.

EDNA

Yes, thank you Scrotum.

LADY ANITA

Well done Scrotum, I must say I fancy some shampoo we seem to have it so rarely these days. Open a bottle of our Perrier-Jouet 89 please.

SCROTUM

Yes madam.

CHAMPAGNE CORK POPS,
CLINKING GLASSES

ANTHONY

I think I'll join you my dear, how about you Reverend.

REVEREND FLOWERDEW

Oh no, this is like the temptation of Christ.

ANTHONY

Come on, live dangerously, it's only a glass of champagne.

REVEREND FLOWERDEW

Oh, alright if you insist.

EDNA

Has anyone seen Ned and Georgina since they went for a walk.

LADY ANITA

The last time I saw them they were disappearing into the maze, why do you ask.

EDNA

Well they've just reappeared looking somewhat flushed and slightly dishevelled.

LADY ANITA

I say, how exciting, I love a scandal. Who would have thought it she looked such a stuffy blue stocking, still I can't say I blame her Ned is rather dishy, isn't he.

THE DINING ROOM DOOR OPENS

AMANDA

Hello everyone you'll be pleased to know that dinner is under control, have I missed anything while I was away.

EDNA

I should say so, we'll tell you later.

THE FRENCH DOORS OPEN

Nice walk, you two.

GEORGINA

Oh yes splendid, I've seen some amazing foliage.

EDNA

Yes, I'm sure you have.

ANTHONY

Champagne anyone.

NED

Yes please and one for Georgina please.

ANTHONY

Amanda, Reverend.

AMANDA

Yes please.

REVEREND FLOWERDEW

Not for me thanks, I think I've had a little to much already, I'm afraid I need to get some fresh air I'm feeling a little whimsy.

THE FRENCH DOORS OPEN

EDNA

Poor old bugger, he'd only had a couple of glasses.

LADY ANITA

I think I'll take this opportunity to go to my room and freshen up before we eat.

THE DINING ROOM DOOR OPENS

LORD ANTHONY

Excellent, I'll hold the fort here. Scrotum, another bottle of bubbly.

SCROTUM

Certainly sir.

CHAMPAGNE CORK POP, CLINKING GLASSES

AMANDA

I've just bought your book, Marrows and how to get a big one, I hadn't realised growing organic vegetables could be so interesting.

NED

That's a coincidence I was just saying to Georgina I had just read your latest book, Cookery Nook. Perhaps we could get together, I'll grow them and you cook them.

AMANDA

Perhaps we could but what would we call the book.

NED

Simple you're known as the sexy chef and I'm known as the hunky gardener the books got to be The Orgasmic Cookbook.

AMANDA

Oh, your such a flirt.

THE DINING ROOM DOOR OPENS

LADY ANITA

Hello again everyone, are we nearly ready to eat, dinner won't be much longer.

THE FRENCH DOOR OPENS

LADY ANITA

Oh Reverend Flowerdew you're back, are you feeling better now

REVEREND FLOWERDEW

Yes I am thank you and may I say what a delightful frock you're wearing. Could you tell me where you bought it I would love to get one for a lady friend of mine.

LADY ANITA

Well actually there's a delightful little shop in Petworth called Mr Spencer Percivals emporium of slightly used goods and ephemera. I know it's rather a long name, the first letters are actually an anagram of MESSAGE SOUP except it's short of an 'S'.

REVEREND FLOWERDEW

You mean it's a second hand shop Lady Anita.

LADY ANITA

Well yes, slightly used. We don't seem to have the cash flow from the estate that we once had, I don't know why, I leave that sort of thing to Lord Anthony.

REVEREND FLOWERDEW

I'm awfully sorry to hear that perhaps one could forego the

donation to next Sundays collection.

LADY ANITA

That's very kind of you Reverend, but I don't think things are quite that bad yet.

A SINGLE GUN SHOT

REVEREND FLOWERDEW

My Lord, what was that.

LADY ANITA

I think it was a gun shot. Oh my God it sounded like it came from the library. Quick Anthony.

LORD ANTHONY

Alright everyone don't panic, Edna come with me.

THE DINING ROOM DOOR OPENS, FOOTSTEPS

EDNA

What do you think happened, was it a gun shot.

THE LIBRARY DOOR OPENS

LORD ANTHONY

I don't know but we're just about to find out. Thomas, Thomas are you alright.

EDNA

My God he's been shot in the chest.

LORD ANTHONY

Can you help him, I'll phone for an ambulance.

EDNA

It's too late for that you'd better get the police he's already dead I'm afraid. Try to keep the others outside, he's not a pretty sight.

LADY ANITA

Anthony, what's happening, is Thomas alright.

ANTHONY

I'm afraid not, stay there don't let anyone in here, call for the police Thomas is dead, he's been shot.

THE DOOR BELL RINGS

LADY ANITA

Alright everyone we'd better go back to the dining room.

REVEREND FLOWERDEW

Are you sure it's safe, there could be a murderer at large.

LADY ANITA

I don't know reverend, but that's what Anthony wants us to do and he always knows best.

FOOTSTEPS, THE DINING ROOM OPENS

SCROTUM

Madam, this is Inspector Frank Williams from Westhampnett CID.

LADY ANITA

I'm sorry Inspector, how did you get here so quickly, I haven't even phoned yet.

INSPECTOR WILLIAMS

Phoned madam, phoned for what. I'm here to see Squadron Leader Thomas Dashfoot Church about missing aviation fuel from the airbase.

LADY ANITA

I'm sorry Inspector but you're too late Thomas is dead he's been murdered, he's in the library with my husband, this way.

FOOTSTEPS, LIBRARY DOOR OPENS

LADY ANITA

Anthony, this is Inspector Frank Williams from Westhampnett CID

INSPECTOR WILLIAMS

Good evening Sir, and you are.

ANTHONY

I'm Lord Anthony Dashfoot Church and this lady is nurse Edna

Seacole.

And I assume this was Squadron Leader Thomas Dashfoot Church.

ANTHONY
Yes Inspector, that's right he was my brother, I can't imagine why anyone would want to kill him.

INSPECTOR WILLIAMS
I take it you don't know anything about the stolen petrol at the airbase.

ANTHONY
No Inspector, nothing at all.

INSPECTOR WILLIAMS
Has anyone touched anything in this room.

ANTHONY
No nothing, this is how we found him, I came in first and Edna was behind me. I realised my brother had been shot and Edna went to assist him but it was too late, he was dead.

INSPECTOR WILLIAMS
So this table is as you found it, with the glass of port and the sleeping pills as they are now.

EDNA
Yes Inspector, Thomas had asked for the port as he was feeling unwell and I gave him the sleeping pills and left the bottle on the table.

INSPECTOR WILLIAMS
And the alarm clock and the gun were on the floor, were they.

EDNA
Yes they were, although the alarm clock was originally on the table.

154

INSPECTOR WILLIAMS

Did either of you put this garden twine on the floor.

ANTHONY

I hadn't even noticed that until you pointed it out, had you Edna.

EDNA

No, not at all.

INSPECTOR WILLIAMS

Thank you, I think that's all I need to see at the moment, if you'll both join the others in the dining room. Please make sure no one leaves I will need to question everybody.

THE LIBRARY DOOR OPENS

ANTHONY

Thank you Inspector.

INSPECTOR WILLIAMS

I'll be with you soon Sir.

FOOTSTEPS

EDNA

Who on earth would want to kill your brother.

ANTHONY

I've no idea, unless it was something to do with the missing petrol.

EDNA

Oh yes, I hadn't thought of that.

THE DINING ROOM DOOR OPENS

ANTHONY

Hello everyone, I've just left Inspector Williams and I'm afraid that none of us can leave as he wants to question everyone. I'm awfully sorry for the inconvenience but in the mean time please remain here.

REVEREND FLOWERDEW
I'd like to say on behalf of all of us how sorry we are about your brother, I'm sure he's gone to a better place.

ANTHONY
Thank you Reverend, I hope you're right.

THE DINING ROOM OPENS

INSPECTOR WILLIAMS
Good evening everybody, I'm Inspector Frank Williams from Westhampnett CID and I'd like to interview you all concerning the death of Squadron Leader Thomas Dashfoot Church. I would like to start with Georgina Archer, I believe you were the first to arrive today.

GEORGINA
Yes I was, I arrived at about half past twelve and I was shown into the dining room where I met Squadron Leader Thomas. I must say I was a little relieved when Ned and Edna arrived about half an hour later.

EDNA
Yes Inspector we arrived together as we had travelled on the same train. I was dying for a drink which I am delighted to say was given to me and we all chatted and drank until about twenty to two when Amanda Bloom arrived. I remember because she asked for an orange juice to drink,

INSPECTOR WILLIAMS
So who was next to arrive.

LADY ANITA
We were, myself and Reverend Flowerdew, I met him in the hall and we came into the dining room together. It must have been just after two o'clock, I chatted to Reverend Flowerdew during which time Thomas groped my bottom which I duly chastised him for. It must have been about two thirty, perhaps a little after when Anthony entered the dining room.

INSPECTOR WILLIAMS
So it's safe to assume you were all gathered here in the dining

room no later than quarter to three.

LORD ANTHONY

That's right Inspector we all had some more drinks and then Thomas became unwell and Nurse Edna and myself took him to the library.

EDNA

I checked his pulse, which was a little fast but nothing to worry about so I gave him some sleeping pills to sedate him and came back into the dining room.

INSPECTOR WILLIAMS

I believe you were a FANY during the war and you offered comfort to the troops.

EDNA

Yes Inspector, I was in the First Aid Nursing Yeomanry, a FANY as you say and I did bring comfort to many of the troops. I don't see what this has to do with Squadron Leader Thomas's death.

INSPECTOR WILLIAMS

Neither do I yet, I was just checking everyones background. So, when you came back into the dining room did Lord Anthony come with you.

EDNA

No, not straight away, he said he would wait until the sedative had taken effect and then joined us shortly afterwards.

INSPECTOR WILLIAMS

Then what happened.

NED

Georgina and I went for a walk in the garden, I think we were the first to leave the room, we went to the maze.

INSPECTOR WILLIAMS

And what did you do there.

NED

Nothing Inspector.

EDNA

That's not what it looked like to us.

GEORGINA

All right, all right, we made love, mad passionate love. I know I look like a rather prim and proper accountant but I do have another side a far more fiery one. Ned and I have been having an affair for ages but we choose to keep it secret for the sake of his wife.

EDNA

Well good luck to you.

GEORGINA

Thank you Edna.

INSPECTOR WILLIAMS

Now Amanda, did you leave the room at any time.

AMANDA

I'm fairly certain I went to the kitchen to check on the meal while Ned and Georgina were in the garden and I came back in just before they came back from the garden.

INSPECTOR WILLIAMS

And where were you when all this was going on Reverend.

REVEREND FLOWERDEW

I was in the dining room all the time until five o'clock when I had to get some fresh air as I was feeling a little whimsy.

INSPECTOR WILLIAMS

You were alone all the time you were outside.

REVEREND FLOWERDEW

Yes Inspector, completely.

LADY ANITA

I left shortly after Reverend Flowerdew left for the garden, I went to freshen up in my room before dinner. I came back to the dining room at about five thirty, at almost the same time as Reverend Flowerdew came back from the garden. I remember because he complimented me on my dress. Then shortly after that we heard the gunshot from the library.

INSPECTOR WILLIAMS

Thank you every one, it seems that the only person not to have left the dining room prior to the murder was Lord Anthony.

LORD ANTHONY

I do believe you're right Inspector.

INSPECTOR WILLIAMS

So everybody except Lord Anthony left the dining room at one time or another giving all of them the opportunity to murder Squadron Leader Thomas and yet the gun shot was heard when you were all together apparently giving everyone an alibi. Something doesn't add up here I need to review the evidence.

I found at the scene a gun with one spent cartridge, an alarm clock and some garden twine. On the table were three celebrity books written by Georgina, Ned and Amanda, what was the point of these books, where they just there to incriminate or to confuse. Even more bizarre was the letter made from newspaper cutting saying Let he that is without sin cast the first stone.

I'm beginning to understand what happened, Squadron Leader Thomas was found in the library seated in a chair shot in the chest but how could this be as everyone was in the dining room at the time.

There is only one explanation and the evidence bears this out. Someone took the gun and wedged it with the books and wound the twine round the trigger and the alarm clock. At the pre set time the alarm clock went off causing it to vibrate off the table and fall to the floor. As it fell the twine tightened round the trigger and the gun went off shooting the sedated Squadron Leader Thomas in the chest. Now we have established the method all we need now is the motive. Who would have wanted to kill Squadron Leader Thomas, was it Georgina and Ned who were afraid he was about to expose their affair.

NED

It wasn't us, I know we didn't want the affair made public but I had made plans to get divorced and make an honest woman of Georgina.

INSPECTOR WILLIAMS

Could it have been Nurse Edna who by her own admission had sedated Squadron Leader Thomas.

EDNA

I may have sedated him but I had nothing to do with his murder I swear.

INSPECTOR WILLIAMS

What of Amanda who had poisoned guests at a previous dinner where Squadron Leader Thomas was present. Was he about to inform Lord Anthony and spoil her chances of future work.

AMANDA

I didn't know the mushrooms were poisonous it was just a tragic mistake.

INSPECTOR WILLIAMS

Even the innocuous Reverend Flowerdew had a motive isn't that right Reverend.

REVEREND FLOWERDEW

I'm afraid you're right, I've been very foolish, I was having an affair with a young girl in my parish.

INSPECTOR WILLIAMS

And how old was she Reverend.

REVEREND FLOWERDEW

Nothing of a sexual nature took place until she was old enough, I assure you. We are deeply in love that's why I sent the note. I knew Squadron Leader Thomas had got wind of my affair and was desperate to plead to his better nature and not expose us.

INSPECTOR WILLIAMS

Which just leaves Lady Anita, how does she fit into this puzzle. She had the opportunity when she went to her room to freshen up and perhaps the continual groping from the letcherous Squadron Leader was the last straw which tipped her over the edge.

LADY ANITA

I wouldn't kill Thomas, I know he always groped me but he'd done it for years, most of the time I just ignored it. Every now and then I would find it a bit tiresome but I certainly wouldn't kill over such a trivial thing.

INSPECTOR WILLIAMS

Well it seems that everyone is innocent and there must be some other explanation and indeed there is. Having examined the library once again I found embedded in the wall another bullet and hidden behind some books this silencer. We now know what happened don't we Lord Anthony.

LORD ANTHONY

I'm sorry Inspector, I don't know what you mean.

INSPECTOR WILLIAMS

Oh, I think you do Sir, for it was you who killed Squadron Leader Thomas.

It was you who drugged your brothers drink causing him to be unwell before you took him to the library. Then again he was given more sedative by the innocent Nurse Edna whom you asked to leave as you waited for the sedative to take effect. As Squadron Leader Thomas became unconscious you fitted the silencer to the gun and shot him in the chest. You quickly hid the silencer, reloaded the gun tying the twine to the trigger and the alarm clock and hurried back to the dining room safe in the knowledge that the gun would fire some hours later when the clock vibrated off the table. Had it not been for the fact that I discovered the bullet embedded in the wall and found the silencer we may have been hanging an innocent person.

LORD ANTHONY

All right Inspector, mea culpa, I'm sorry, I'm so sorry. I'm afraid the estate was losing money hand over fist and I couldn't see a way out. Then Thomas told me his liver was packing up, he knew the signs from friends of his who'd gone the same way. He always was a drunken letch and I'm afraid I saw my opportunity. I took out a massive life insurance policy on him and obviously you know the rest. It didn't seem that bad he was going to die anyway, I just couldn't face loosing Westhampnett House it's been in the family for generations.

INSPECTOR WILLIAMS

A very sad situation indeed Sir but I'm afraid, Lord Anthony Dashfoot Church I'm arresting you for the murder of your brother Squadron Leader Thomas Dashfoot Church. Please come with me.

BANGED TO RIGHTS

THE DOOR OPENS AND CLOSES

DS TONY WALTERS
Thank's for coming in Mr Callow, if you take a seat PAUSE the other side of the table, if you would Sir.

DENNIS CALLOW
Do you have any news Sergeant.

DS TONY WALTERS
Not exactly Sir, just take a seat, would you like a drink, tea perhaps.

DENNIS CALLOW
No thanks, I'm fine.

THE DOOR OPENS AND CLOSES

DS TONY WALTERS
Hello Sir.

DCI JOHN SPENCER
Sergeant, Mr Callow.

DS TONY WALTERS
I'm Detective Sergeant Tony Walters and I have to inform you this interview will be taped.

TAPE MACHINE CLICKS ON.

I'm Detective Sergeant Tony Walters of Woodburn Hill Police Station, also present is Detective Chief Inspector John Spencer. For the purpose of the tape could you please confirm your full name.

DENNIS CALLOW
Me.

DS TONY WALTERS
Yes Sir, please.

DENNIS CALLOW
I don't understand.

DS TONY WALTERS
> Your full name, please Sir.

DENNIS CALLOW
> My name is Dennis Callow.

DS TONY WALTERS
> And your address and date of birth, please Sir.

DENNIS CALLOW
> My address is 27 Lexham Road, Woodburn Hill, London and my date of birth is the twenty second of November nineteen eighty.

DS TONY WALTERS
> Also present is Detective Chief Inspector John Spencer. Can you confirm for the purpose of the tape that there are no other persons present in the room Sir.

DENNIS CALLOW
> HESITANTLY. There is no one else here.

DS TONY WALTERS
> It's Friday the tenth of July two thousand and nine and it's now one thirty and this interview is taking place in Woodburn Hill police station. I now need to caution you Sir, you do not have to say anything, but it may harm your defence if you do not mention when questioned something which you may later rely on in court. Anything you do say may be given in evidence. Do you under stand the caution I have just given you.

DENNIS CALLOW
> I do, but I don't understand why.

DS TONY WALTERS
> I need to point out to you Sir that you have the right to a solicitor should you want one.

DENNIS CALLOW
> I don't want one, I've done nothing wrong.

DS TONY WALTERS
Excellent Sir, then Detective Chief Inspector John Spencer has a few questions for you.

DENNIS CALLOW
I still don't understand have you found Sharon, is this what this is all about.

DCI JOHN SPENCER
No Sir, we haven't found her, that's what this is all about.

DENNIS CALLOW
Why are you wasting time questioning me, a little girl is missing somewhere out there, you should be looking for her not questioning me, I've told you everything already.

DCI JOHN SPENCER
Yes Sir, but we need to go over it once more.

DENNIS CALLOW
Ok, I got a call from Brenda on Wednesday afternoon to say Sharon hadn't come home from school and was she with me.

DS TONY WALTERS
Brenda, she's your girlfriend.

DENNIS CALLOW
Yes, I've told you this before, we've been together for nearly two years now.

DS TONY WALTERS
So Sharon's not your child.

DENNIS CALLOW
Of course not, although I think of her as mine

DS TONY WALTERS
Yours, Sir.

DENNIS CALLOW
Yes Sergeant, like she was my own child, we are very close.

DS TONY WALTERS

And what does Brenda think of this.

DENNIS CALLOW

She's fine, what else would she be. I had a little sister when I was young but she died of meningitis so I appreciate how precious Sharon is and Brenda knows it.

DCI JOHN SPENCER

So she failed to come home from school on Wednesday afternoon and Brenda phoned, then what did you do.

DENNIS CALLOW

Nothing I was on the way to a kids party, I told her I would do the party and then come home. I thought Sharon was probably at one of her friends and had forgotten to let us know.

DCI JOHN SPENCER

Doing a kids party, Sir.

DENNIS CALLOW

Yes Inspector I'm a childrens entertainer, I'm Mr Bunny Fones, it's a joke on Funny Bones. I pull rabbits from hats and do magic and balloons.

DS TONY WALTERS

So your girlfriends' daughter goes missing and you're too busy to be by her side.

DENNIS CALLOW

It's not like that, Sharon's very capable I was sure she would turn up and as soon as the party was over I went home to Brenda.

DS TONY WALTERS

Home Sir, that's not the address you gave as home.

DENNIS CALLOW

Well I think of it as home, I've spent most of my time there this last year or so, it's just that if I move in they loose their benefits.

DCI JOHN SPENCER

So, you're willing to lie about benefits, what else are you willing to lie about.

DENNIS CALLOW

Nothing Inspector, nothing, I've told you the truth from the beginning. If you want to shop us for benefit fraud, go on, at the moment I don't give a damn what happens as long as we get Sharon back.

DCI JOHN SPENCER

You went on television on Thursday with Brenda to publicise Sharons disappearance.

DENNIS CALLOW

Yes, we did, what else would you expect us to do.

DCI JOHN SPENCER

Nothing Sir, except since your television appearance we've been inundated with calls from concerned parents who've had you at their childrens parties. Some have even suggested that you seemed to have an unhealthy liking for children and you may be a paedophile.

DENNIS CALLOW

A paedophile, how dare you accuse me of being a paedophile, I love children.

DS TONY WALTERS

Perhaps too much Sir.

DENNIS CALLOW

If you'd lost your sister when she was six you wouldn't talk to me like this, every child is precious.

DCI JOHN SPENCER

Indeed Sir, is it not in the Bible, suffer little children to come unto me.

DENNIS CALLOW

I don't know, all I do know is that I want Sharon back safe and sound.

DS TONY WALTERS

That's what we all want Dennis, you don't mind if I call you Dennis do you.

DENNIS CALLOW

No I don't mind.

DS TONY WALTERS

I have to inform you Dennis that during a search of your flat we found a number of photographs of Sharon.

DENNIS CALLOW

Of course you did I'm going out with her mother.

DCI JOHN SPENCER

I think what my Sergeant is trying to say Dennis is that we found an unhealthy number of photographs of this vunerable young girl.

DENNIS CALLOW

It's not like that, I think of her as my daughter.

DCI JOHN SPENCER

You also keep her knickers in your flat don't you Dennis.

DS TONY WALTERS

Photographs, young girls knickers, what's that all about Dennis, some sort of sexual gratification.

PAUSE. Do you masturbate Dennis.

DENNIS CALLOW

No, no this is all wrong, you've got it all wrong.

DS TONY WALTERS

Have we Dennis, if we've got it so wrong what's your explanation.

DENNIS CALLOW

I take pictures of her because I love her, I love her as if she was my own. Do you have children Inspector.

169

DCI JOHN SPENCER

I do Dennis, but I don't have an excessive number of photos of my daughter and I certainly don't keep her knickers in my bedroom.

DENNIS CALLOW

They must have got mixed up in the washing and I took them home by mistake.

DS TONY WALTERS

And you didn't take them back, Dennis, you must have had plenty of opportunities.

DENNIS CALLOW

I suppose I must have done Sergeant, but it didn't seem that important at the time.

DS TONY WALTERS

Well, it's important now isn't it Dennis.

DENNIS CALLOW

I suppose so, yes.

DS TONY WALTERS

I think this is a good time to stop now, to give you time to think how important these things are. Interview suspended at three thirty.

DCI JOHN SPENCER

My Sergeant will take you back to the cells.

DS TONY WALTERS

Just before I take you down Dennis and while the tape is stopped perhaps I can give you some words of advice.

DENNIS CALLOW

Some, what.

DS TONY WALTERS

Some advice Dennis. I know you've never been inside before so I suggest that if you do know anything, which may help you, now would be a good time to tell us. If you do go inside for this,

Dennis, you'll be a nonce, a paedophile, do you realise what that means. If your lucky and you get protective custody you'll be banged up in solitary confinement for twenty three hours a day in a room the size of your bathroom. If you don't get protective custody, have you any idea what happens to a nonce in prison, it's your worst nightmare Dennis. Take this little break to have a think, if you are innocent now's the time to tell us, before it's too late.

THE DOOR OPENS AND CLOSES.

TIME PASSES

THE DOOR OPENS AND CLOSES

DS TONY WALTERS
In you go Dennis, I hope you're feeling better now you've had time to think.

DCI JOHN SPENCER
Take a seat Dennis.

THE TAPE MACHINE CLICKS ON

DS TONY WALTERS
It's Friday the tenth of July two thousand and nine, interview resumed at four thirty. Present are Detective Sergeant Tony Walters, Detective Chief Inspector John Spencer and Dennis Callow. May I remind you Dennis that you are still under caution.

DENNIS CALLOW
You can't do this to me, it's not fair I'm innocent.

DS TONY WALTERS
Then prove it Dennis.

DENNIS CALLOW
I can't, I can't. For Gods sake help me I've done nothing wrong.

DCI JOHN SPENCER
Alright Dennis, if you're telling the truth whose not telling the truth.

DS TONY WALTERS
You say you've known Brenda for two years.

DENNIS CALLOW
Yes.

DS TONY WALTERS
And what did you know of her prior to that.

DENNIS CALLOW
Well, nothing much, what could I know before we met. She's a kind and caring person and a wonderful mother to Sharon.

DS TONY WALTERS
She was cautioned for assaulting Sharons dad and she was lucky to get away with a caution.

DENNIS CALLOW
Yes, but he was put away for grievous bodily harm to her, he was a nasty vicious piece of work.

DS TONY WALTERS
We are aware of this Dennis but he wasn't the one accused of being a paedophile.

DENNIS CALLOW
Wrongly accused.

DS TONY WALTERS
So you say, Dennis, so you say.

DCI JOHN SPENCER
Ok Dennis, lets assume you're telling the truth, then where is Sharon.

DENNIS CALLOW
Perhaps her dads got her, he always threatened revenge when he was put away.

DS TONY WALTERS
He'd have a hard job Dennis he's still in Wandsworth nick and he's not due for release until August.

DENNIS CALLOW

No no no, that's wrong he's out I've seen him, I'm sure I've seen him.

DS TONY WALTERS

For the purpose of the tape Detective Sergeant Tony Walters is leaving the room.

THE DOOR OPENS AND CLOSES

DCI JOHN SPENCER

Why didn't you say this before Dennis.

DENNIS CALLOW

I just assumed you must have known, surely you knew.

THE DOOR OPENS AND CLOSES

DCI JOHN SPENCER

For the purpose of the tape Detective Sergeant Tony Walters has re entered the room.

DS TONY WALTERS

You're not going to believe this Sir, there's good news and bad news.

DCI JOHN SPENCER

What's the bad news.

DS TONY WALTERS

He's out, he got early release the computer hadn't updated, I can't believe it.

DCI JOHN SPENCER

And the good news.

DS TONY WALTERS

He's just been nicked for drunken driving and Sharon was in the car.

DENNIS CALLOW

Is she safe, please tell me she's alright.

DS TONY WALTERS

Yes Dennis it seems she's alright.

DENNIS CALLOW

Thank God for that, I told you he was an evil bastard.

DCI JOHN SPENCER

Well it seems you were right Dennis, I'm sorry we got it wrong but you have to understand we had no option.

DENNIS CALLOW

No option, no option, your not the one who was arrested as a suspected paedophile. Do you know what that means, do you. I'll never work as Mr Bunny Fones again, the job I loved. Who's going to employ me ever again, oh yes Mr Bunny Fones, he's the paedophile, I'll never be able to work with children ever again, you've ruined my life.

DCI JOHN SPENCER

You were only brought in for questioning, you're an innocent man.

DENNIS CALLOW

I know that as well as you do Inspector but how many of my future employers are going to remember I was innocent, all they'll remember is I was hauled in as a paedophile. Any way, all I want to do now is be with Brenda and Sharon, I just want to leave.

DCI JOHN SPENCER

And you can Dennis. I'm sorry you had to go through this but you've got to understand we had no option. We were just doing our job.

THE DOOR OPENS AND CLOSES

Printed in Great Britain
by Amazon